Order in the Court

A Mock Trial Simulation

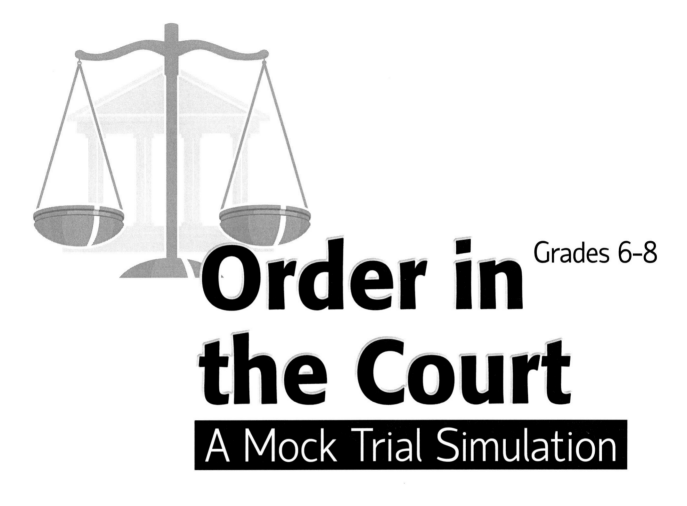

Grades 6-8

Order in the Court

A Mock Trial Simulation

Darcy O. Blauvelt & Richard G. Cote

 Routledge
Taylor & Francis Group

NEW YORK AND LONDON

First published in 2012 by Prufrock Press Inc.

Published in 2021 by Routledge
605 Third Avenue, New York, NY 10017
2 Park Square, Milton Park, Abingdon, Oxon OX14 4RN

Routledge is an imprint of the Taylor & Francis Group, an informa business

Copyright © 2012 by Taylor & Francis Group

Production Design by Raquel Trevino

ISBN: 9781032142050 (hbk)
ISBN: 9781593638290 (pbk)

DOI: 10.4324/9781003236955

TABLE OF CONTENTS

Introduction

Background

Gifted program directors, resource specialists, and—perhaps most importantly—general education classroom teachers who struggle with the challenge of providing appropriate services to students of high potential in the traditional classroom will be interested in these Interactive Discovery-Based Units for High-Ability Learners. The units encourage students to use nontraditional methods to demonstrate learning.

Any given curriculum is composed of two distinct, though not separate, entities: content and context. In every classroom environment, there are forces at work that define the content to be taught. These forces may take the form of high-stakes tests or local standards. But in these Interactive Discovery-Based Units for High-Ability Learners, the context of a traditional classroom is reconfigured so that students are provided with a platform from which to demonstrate academic performance and understanding that are not shown through traditional paper-and-pencil methods. This way, teachers go home smiling and students go home tired at the end of the school day.

DOI: 10.4324/9781003236955-1

C = C + C
Curriculum = Content + Context

In March of 2005, the Further Steps Forward Project (FSFP) was established and funded under the Jacob K. Javits Gifted and Talented Students Education Program legislation. The project had a two-fold, long-range mission:

- The first goal was to identify, develop, and test identification instruments specific to special populations of the gifted, focusing on the economically disadvantaged.
- The second goal was to create, deliver, and promote professional development focused on minority and underserved populations of the gifted, especially the economically disadvantaged.

The result was the Student Context Rubric (SCR), which is included in each of the series' eight units. The SCR, discussed in further depth in the Appendix, is a rubric that a teacher or specialist uses to evaluate a student in five areas: engagement, creativity, synthesis, interpersonal ability, and verbal communication. When used in conjunction with the units in this series, the SCR provides specialists with an excellent tool for identifying students of masked potential—students who are gifted but are not usually recognized—and it gives general education teachers the language necessary to advocate for these students when making recommendations for gifted and additional services. The SCR also provides any teacher with a tool for monitoring and better understanding student behaviors.

Using best practices from the field of gifted education as a backdrop, we viewed students through the lens of the following core beliefs as we developed each unit:

- instrumentation must be flexible in order to recognize a variety of potentials;
- curricula must exist that benefit all students while also making clear which students would benefit from additional services; and
- identification processes and services provided by gifted programming must be integral to the existing curriculum; general education teachers cannot view interventions and advocacy as optional.

These eight contextually grounded units, two in each of the four core content areas (language arts, social studies, math, and science), were developed to serve as platforms from which middle school students could strut their stuff, displaying their knowledge and learning in practical, fun contexts. Two of the units (*Ecopolis* and *What's Your Opinion?*) were awarded the prestigious National Association for Gifted Children (NAGC) Curriculum Award in 2009. Over the span of 3 years, we—and other general education teachers—taught all of the units multiple times to measure their effectiveness as educational vehicles and to facilitate dynamic professional development experiences.

The FSFP documented that in 11 of 12 cases piloted in the 2008–2009 school year, middle school students showed statistically significant academic gains. In particular, those students who were underperforming in the classroom showed great progress. Furthermore, there were statistically significant improvements in students' perceptions of their classroom environments in terms of innovation and involvement. Finally, the contextually grounded units in this series can be used as springboards for further study and projects, offering teachers opportunities for cross-disciplinary collaboration.

Administrators, teachers, and gifted specialists will gain from this series a better sense of how to develop and use contextualized units—not only in the regular education classroom, but also in gifted programming.

How to Use the Units

Every lesson in the units includes an introductory section listing the concepts covered, suggested materials, grade-level expectations, and student objectives. This section also explains how the lesson is introduced, how students demonstrate recognition of the concepts, how they apply their knowledge, and how they solve related problems. The lesson plans provided, while thorough, also allow for differentiation and adaptation. Depending on how much introduction and review of the material students need, you may find that some lessons take more or less time than described. We have used these units in 50-minute class periods, but the subparts of the lesson—introducing the material, recognizing the concepts, applying knowledge, and solving a problem—allow for adaptability in terms of scheduling. The "Additional Notes" for each lesson provide further tips, flag potential problem areas, and offer suggestions for extending the lesson.

This series offers many contextual units from which to choose; however, we do not recommend using them exclusively. In our research, we have found that students who are constantly involved in contextual learning become immune to its benefits. We recommend, therefore, that you vary the delivery style of material across the school year. For most classes, spacing out three contextual units over the course of the year produces optimal results.

These units may be used in place of other curriculum. However, if you find that your students are stumbling over a specific skill as they progress through a unit, do not hesitate to take a day off from the unit and instead use direct instruction to teach that skill. This will help to ensure that students are successful as they move forward. It is necessary for students to be frustrated and challenged, as this frustration serves as the impetus of learning—yet they must not be so frustrated that they give up. Throughout the unit, you must find the delicate balance between providing challenges for your students and overwhelming them.

The Role of the Teacher

A contextual unit is a useful vehicle both for engaging your students and for assessing their abilities. As a teacher, your role changes in a contextual unit. Rather than being the driving force, you are the behind-the-scenes producer. The students are the drivers of this creative vehicle. If you are used to direct instruction methods of teaching, you will need to make a conscious choice not to run the show. Although this may feel a bit uncomfortable for you in the beginning, the rewards for your students will prove well worth the effort. As you become more comfortable with the process, you will find that this teaching method is conducive to heightening student engagement and learning while also allowing you to step back and observe your students at work.

Group Dynamics

Cooperation plays a key role in this unit. Small-group work is fraught with challenges for all of us. Creating groups that will be able to accomplish their objectives—groups whose members will fulfill their roles—takes some forethought. Keep in mind that sometimes the very act of working through any issues that arise may be the most powerful learning tool of all. Before beginning the unit, you should discuss with students the importance of working together and assigning tasks to ensure that work is distributed and completed fairly and equally.

Preparation and Pacing

Deciding on a timeline is very important as you plan the implementation of the unit. You know your students better than anyone else does. Some students may be more successful when they are immersed in the unit, running it every day for 3 weeks. Others would benefit from having some days off to get the most out of their experiences.

Every classroom is different. Students possess different sets of prior knowledge, learning strategies, and patterns. This means that as the teacher, you must make decisions about how much of the material you will introduce prior to the unit, whether you will provide occasional traditional instruction throughout the unit, how many days off you will give students, and how much your students will discover on their own throughout the course of the unit. For example, in this social studies unit, students play the roles of witnesses and lawyers, employing both persuasive writing and public speaking skills. You may decide to review the components of persuasive writing in more detail to complement the unit, or you might focus on public speaking for a few days in order to get students more comfortable getting up in front of the class before beginning the trial. This book is not meant to provide exact instructions; in every lesson, there is wiggle room in terms of how you work alongside students to enable them to demonstrate learning.

Also, you should feel free to use materials other than those suggested. If there is a topic or source that is highly relevant for your students, then it might be worthwhile for you to compile research sites, articles, and other materials about the topic in order to provide your students a degree of real-world involvement.

Using these units is a bit like using a recipe in the kitchen. The first time you use one of the units, you may want to use it just as it is written. Each successive time you use it, however, you may choose to adjust the ratios and substitute ingredients to suit your own tastes. The more you personalize the units to your students' situations and preferences, the more engaged they will be—and the same goes for you as the teacher.

Grade-Level Expectations

All of our units are aligned with New Hampshire's Grade-Level Expectations. These state requirements are similar to many states' GLEs, and we hope that they will be useful for you. For each lesson, we have listed the applicable New Hampshire GLEs in a format that illustrates which learning objectives students are meeting by completing the given tasks.

Adaptability

"Organized chaos" is a phrase often used to describe a contextual classroom. The students are not sitting at their desks and quietly taking notes while the teacher delivers information verbally. A classroom full of students actively engaged in their learning and creatively solving real-world problems is messy, but highly productive. Every teacher has his or her own level of tolerance for this type of chaos, and you may find yourself needing days off occasionally. Organization is an essential ingredient for success in a contextual unit. For example, you will need a place in your classroom where students can access paperwork. It is important to think through timeframes and allow for regular debriefing sessions.

You will also want to develop a personalized method for keeping track of who is doing what. Some students will be engaged from the start, but others you will need to prod and encourage to become involved. This will be especially true if your students are unfamiliar with this type of contextual learning. There are always a few students who try to become invisible so that classmates will do their work for them. Others may be Tom Sawyers, demonstrating their interpersonal skills by persuading peers to complete their work. You will want to keep tabs on both of these types of students so that you can maximize individual student learning. Some teachers have students keep journals, others use daily exit card strategies, and others use checklists. Again, many aspects of how to use these units are up to you.

It is difficult in a busy classroom to collect detailed behavioral data about your students, but one advantage of contextual learning is that it is much easier to spend observation time in the classroom when you are not directly running the show! If you have the luxury of having an assistant or classroom visitor who can help you collect anecdotal data, then we recommend keeping some sort of log of student behavior. What has worked well for us has been to create a list of students' pictures, with a blank box next to each picture in which behaviors can be recorded.

Contextual units require the teacher to do a considerable amount of work prior to beginning the unit, but once you have put everything into place, the students take over and you can step back and observe as they work, solve problems, and learn.

Unit Overview

This unit was originally based on the authentic performance assessment "Mock Trial" by Drs. Tonya Moon, Carolyn Callahan, Catherine Brighton, and Carol A. Tomlinson under the auspices of The National Research Center on the Gifted and Talented. The focus of the unit is to ensure that students possess the necessary skills to complete this performance, including grade-level reading and persuasive writing skills. Students will need a basic understanding of established courtroom procedures, as well as some role-play experience. This unit gives students the opportunity to synthesize information from various content areas and to hone their teamwork skills.

The preliminary weeks of the unit are spent developing the required knowledge base of courtroom roles and procedures. The students work in teams to understand the chronology and responsibilities of several practice trials before participating in the trial of *Ms. Petunia Pig v. Mr. B.B. Wolf*, a trial based on the classic fairy tale "The Three Little Pigs." Students should gain a sense of the importance of teamwork, time management, and preparation.

Once the students feel comfortable with these processes and procedures, they are introduced to the final project topic, prompts, and rubrics, at which point final trial preparation begins in earnest, culminating in a full mock trial enactment. This

DOI: 10.4324/9781003236955-2

final trial addresses music piracy, a topic we have found extremely relevant in students' everyday lives.

We often use this unit in the fall. Due to its high level of engagement, it is useful as an icebreaker unit once classroom patterns and norms have been established. Often, students we would not have suspected of being enthusiastic actors have stolen the show and gained approval from their peers via a strong portrayal of B. B. Wolf or a dominating performance as a prosecutor!

Unit Outline

We designed these lessons to be used during 50-minute class periods. Depending on the extent to which you need to review concepts with your students, and the amount of time you decide to devote to particular activities, some of these lessons may take fewer or more days than indicated. We have tried to note how many days each lesson will take to complete.

Lesson 1

Students participate in an activity that introduces them to terms and roles associated with the court. This activity is run in the round robin style, with groups adding on to other groups' definitions of key terms and phrases. This is useful not only for determining prior knowledge, but also for encouraging students to discuss unfamiliar concepts. The class synthesizes students' knowledge and instruction and agrees on appropriate definitions.

Lesson 2

Terms and roles used in court are introduced by having students identify dialogue used in court proceedings. The sequence of trial events is reinforced by hav-

DOI: 10.4324/9781003236955-3

ing students role-play using provided dialogues to simulate parts of two trials: one dealing with a pizza parlor robbery, and the other dealing with a streetfight between a dog and a pack of cats. (*Note:* This lesson requires 2 days.)

Lesson 3

Students hear or read a familiar fairytale, "The Three Little Pigs," and then consider the fairytale in terms of legal terms. Student are assigned courtroom roles as witnesses, lawyers, and bailiffs, and then students demonstrate their understanding of courtroom procedures by preparing to stage the trial of *Ms.Petunia Pig v. Mr. B.B. Wolf.* (*Note:* This lesson requires 3 days.)

Lesson 4

Students demonstrate a growing understanding of trial procedures and the specifics of the case by performing the trial in their assigned roles. Students are assessed based on three elements: their performance on preparation based on their assigned roles, their trial performance (a rubric for assessment is provided), and their jury performance in terms of their attentiveness, engagement, and participation in deliberations. The trial is run twice so that when the first team is trying the case, the second team acts as the jury, and vice versa. (*Note:* This lesson requires 2 days.)

Lesson 5

Students develop a deeper understanding of court processes by analyzing the roles and conditions surrounding various cases, first individually, and then in groups. We recommend that students be given two class periods to complete this process. This way, on the first day, students can work by themselves, and on the second day, students can be put into groups according to which cases they analyzed. After comparing notes, groups may present their cases to the class. (*Note:* This lesson requires 2 days.)

Lesson 6

Students have a final opportunity to demonstrate their understanding of courtroom procedures, courtroom roles, and legal strategies. Final trial roles are assigned, and students are given class time to prepare their cases. This final trial deals with sound recording piracy and incorporates actual United States copyright law, lending more relevance to this trial than to the previous one. Students are assessed based on two rubrics—a general performance rubric, and a role-specific rubric. Each student plays both a courtroom role and the role of a jury member. (*Note:* This lesson requires 5 days.)

Lesson 7

Following a class debriefing, students are given the opportunity to assess their own performances and to reflect upon the unit.

Glossary

For the purposes of this unit, the following definitions will be used.

- **Bailiff:** a court employee who keeps the trial running according to established rules and regulations
- **Closing Statement:** a summarization of the case from each side's point of view
- **Cross-Examination:** a questioning of the witnesses by the opposing side; when cross-examining, lawyers use direct, yes-no questions
- **Defendant:** the person accused of wrongdoing
- **Defense:** a team that may include one or more lawyers who argue the case from the point of view of the defendant
- **Direct Examination:** a questioning of the witnesses by their own lawyers, who use open-ended questions to enable the witnesses to tell the complete story
- **Eyewitness:** a person who actually saw some or all of the events pertaining to the case
- **Expert Witness:** a person who is recognized by the court as an expert in the field which he or she will testify about (e.g., DNA testing)

DOI: 10.4324/9781003236955-4

- **Jury:** a group of people (usually 12) who have no connection to the case and are thus impartial
- **Opening Statement:** a statement, made by both the defense and the prosecution, that outlines the facts of the case
- **Plaintiff:** the person who is bringing the suit against the defendant
- **Proof:** a witness's testimony or tangible evidence supporting either the guilt or innocence of the defendant
- **Prosecution:** a team that may include one or more lawyers who argue the case from the point of view of the plaintiff
- **Witness:** a person who has been called by the prosecution or the defense to provide information pertaining to the case

Lesson 1

Concepts

- Opening and closing statements
- Direct examination
- Cross-examination
- Defense and prosecution
- Jury of peers

Materials

- Round Robin sheets (pp. 15–22)
- Markers (eight different colors)
- Clipboards (optional)

Student Objective

The student is introduced to the terms and roles used in a court of law, and the class's prior knowledge of the subject is determined using a group activity.

Introduction

Post the Round Robin sheets around the room or tape them to the blackboard. Introduce the terms by reading the sheets aloud, and then divide the students into eight small groups. Assign one of the terms and a different colored marker to each group.

Recognition

Each team takes 1–3 minutes to write down everything it knows about the term on the provided sheet. When time is called, the groups rotate and move on to the next sheet, reading and adding on to the previous teams' definitions. The groups progress through the sheets until they have visited all eight sheets.

DOI: 10.4324/9781003236955-5

Application

Through presentation and discussion, the students learn the terms.
1. When each group has returned to its original sheet, students read through what other groups wrote and decide how best to define the term.
2. Each team shares its definition with the class.
3. You may refine, reframe, or clarify the students' definitions as necessary.

Problem Solving

Together, the class works to understand and contextualize the terms.
1. The class comes to a consensus about definitions.
2. Students brainstorm about how the terms fit together in a court of law.
3. Students organize the terms according to role and sequence.

Grade-Level Expectations

The student:
• Identifies the meanings of unfamiliar words by using strategies to unlock meaning.
• Shows breadth of vocabulary knowledge, demonstrating understanding of word meanings or relationships by the use of words in context.
• Demonstrates initial understanding of an informational text by organizing information to show understanding.
• Uses comprehension strategies before, during, and after reading an informational text.

Additional Notes

• This lesson is intended to serve as a springboard to help introduce or review the necessary terms of the unit. It is important to assure the students that it is fine if they are unfamiliar with these terms. They should simply do their best and ask questions.
• It is up to you to determine how much time students will need at each station in the round robin activity. At the first station, the students will be brainstorming and writing only. At subsequent stations, they will need to read previous groups' definitions, but as they go along, fewer additions will need to be made to the definitions.
• If students feel that previous groups' definitions are incorrect, they should not be allowed to alter them. However, they may offer constructive feedback in their own sections (e.g., "The blue group said that the prosecutor was 'the bad guy,' but we say that the prosecutor is not necessarily bad and is just doing his or her job").
• When we run this unit, we like to keep the sheets and then review them with students at the close of the unit. This way, they have tangible proof of how much they have learned.

OPENING STATEMENT

Directions: Discuss the above term with your group members. Read what other groups have written about this term, and add to and comment on their definition(s). Do not write directly on any other group's definition. Use the back of this sheet if necessary.

Group 1: _____

_____

Group 2: _____

_____

Group 3: _____

_____

Group 4: _____

_____

Group 5: _____

_____

Group 6: _____

_____

Group 7: _____

_____

Group 8: _____

_____

Name:_____ Date: _____

CLOSING STATEMENT

Directions: Discuss the above term with your group members. Read what other groups have written about this term, and add to and comment on their definition(s). Do not write directly on any other group's definition. Use the back of this sheet if necessary.

Group 1: _____

_____

Group 2: _____

_____

Group 3: _____

_____

Group 4: _____

_____

Group 5: _____

_____

Group 6: _____

_____

Group 7: _____

_____

Group 8: _____

_____

Name:_____ Date: _____

DIRECTION EXAMINATION OF WITNESS

Directions: Discuss the above term with your group members. Read what other groups have written about this term, and add to and comment on their definition(s). Do not write directly on any other group's definition. Use the back of this sheet if necessary.

Group 1: _____

_____

Group 2: _____

_____

Group 3: _____

_____

Group 4: _____

_____

Group 5: _____

_____

Group 6: _____

_____

Group 7: _____

_____

Group 8: _____

_____

CROSS-EXAMINATION OF WITNESS

Directions: Discuss the above term with your group members. Read what other groups have written about this term, and add to and comment on their definition(s). Do not write directly on any other group's definition. Use the back of this sheet if necessary.

Group 1: _____

_____

Group 2: _____

_____

Group 3: _____

_____

Group 4: _____

_____

Group 5: _____

_____

Group 6: _____

_____

Group 7: _____

_____

Group 8: _____

_____

DEFENSE

Directions: Discuss the above term with your group members. Read what other groups have written about this term, and add to and comment on their definition(s). Do not write directly on any other group's definition. Use the back of this sheet if necessary.

Group 1: _____

_____

Group 2: _____

_____

Group 3: _____

_____

Group 4: _____

_____

Group 5: _____

_____

Group 6: _____

_____

Group 7: _____

_____

Group 8: _____

_____

PROSECUTION

. . . .

Directions: Discuss the above term with your group members. Read what other groups have written about this term, and add to and comment on their definition(s). Do not write directly on any other group's definition. Use the back of this sheet if necessary.

Group 1: _____

_____

Group 2: _____

_____

Group 3: _____

_____

Group 4: _____

_____

Group 5: _____

_____

Group 6: _____

_____

Group 7: _____

_____

Group 8: _____

_____

DEFENDANT AND PLAINTIFF

Directions: Discuss the above terms with your group members. (Note that these are two different terms.) Read what other groups have written about these terms, and add to and comment on their definitions. Do not write directly on any other group's definition. Use the back of this sheet if necessary.

Group 1: _____

_____

Group 2: _____

_____

Group 3: _____

_____

Group 4: _____

_____

Group 5: _____

_____

Group 6: _____

_____

Group 7: _____

_____

Group 8: _____

_____

JUDGE AND JURY

Directions: Discuss the above terms with your group members. (Note that these are two different terms.) Read what other groups have written about these terms, and add to and comment on their definitions. Do not write directly on any other group's definition. Use the back of this sheet if necessary.

Group 1: _____

_____

Group 2: _____

_____

Group 3: _____

_____

Group 4: _____

_____

Group 5: _____

_____

Group 6: _____

_____

Group 7: _____

_____

Group 8: _____

_____

Lesson 2

Concepts

- Prosecution
- Defense
- Witnesses
- Judge
- Jury
- Plaintiff
- Defendant

Materials

- Court Role-Play Dialogue Guide sheets (Case 1, pp. 26–29; Case 2, pp. 33–36)
- Court Role-Play Dialogue cards (Case 1, pp. 30–32; Case 2, pp. 37–38)

Student Objective

The student, through observing and role-playing court situations, reinforces his or her understanding of the terms and roles used in court.

Introduction

Introduce the roles that students will play in the trial, and explain and discuss them as necessary. The first trial concerns a robbery at a pizza parlor. The roles are for the bailiff, the prosecution, the defense, and two witnesses for the prosecution (a detective and the pizza parlor's owner). The second trial concerns a canine defendant named Fido who argues that an attack incident against a group of tabby cats was provoked and was committed in self-defense. The roles here are for the bailiff,

DOI: 10.4324/9781003236955-6

the prosecution, the defense, and two expert witnesses, one each for the prosecution and the defense.

Recognition

Students review the terms from the Round Robin sheets in Lesson 1 and then discuss their roles using those terms (e.g., "The defending and prosecuting attorneys make opening statements").

Application

Students identify the terms in context.
1. Students review the Court Role-Play Dialogue cards provided.
2. Students identify the speakers of each card according to their knowledge of terms and roles.
3. Students read cards aloud in order.

Problem Solving

Students become comfortable with the terms by role-playing.
1. Students role-play the sample trial by reading aloud the provided sentences on either the cards or the sheet.
2. Terms are reviewed as necessary.

Grade-Level Expectations

The student:
*   Identifies the meanings of unfamiliar words by using strategies to unlock meaning.
*   Shows breadth of vocabulary knowledge, demonstrating understanding of word meanings or relationships by the use of words in context.
*   Demonstrates initial understanding of informational texts by organizing information to show understanding.
*   Uses comprehension strategies before, during, and after reading informational text.

Additional Notes

*   In this activity, students will be expected to work through a mock trial using a provided script copied onto individual cards. Students should put the cards in order and determine which speakers in a trial should have each card. You may choose to run this activity in various ways depending on what you want your students to accomplish. The activity works well with the whole class,

but you could also put students into small groups. You could pass out the provided cards without telling students the speakers or the order in which the dialogue occurs. This way, it will fall to students to deduce who the speakers of the dialogue must be, as well as to determine the sequence of the lines. After they have done this, you may assign roles and have them enact the trial, becoming more comfortable with courtroom language and the trial order. Alternatively, you might assign roles and then distribute cards to the corresponding speakers. This way, students know who is saying what, but they still have to figure out the logical order of the dialogue based on what they have learned about courtroom proceedings. Students can then run through the trial as in the first option, familiarizing themselves with the language and the sequence. A final option is to give students all of the information and simply discuss the context clues with them prior to doing a role-play of the trial. In this case, you could provide either the cards (with explanations) or the comprehensive guide to students.

- Likewise, you can code the cards in whatever manner best helps you keep track of roles and sequence according to how you are structuring the activity (we have provided our own chosen color and label method). Even if you do not provide any information to work from, we have found that students are fairly oblivious to the codes we write on the backs of cards.

- You can further expand the number of speaking parts by having more than one prosecutor and defender.

- We have tried to make the role-playing parts in this book gender neutral wherever possible so that students feel comfortable playing any role. (In the case involving Little Red Riding Hood and the Big Bad Wolf, we retained the traditional gender roles of the characters, although you can feel free to take liberties with casting!)

- In the trials in this book, the provided materials contain many opportunities for students to point out illogical arguments or holes in reasoning. In the second trial in this lesson, for instance, the position of the prosecution (representing the Tabby Group, a pack of cats) is that because cats are smarter than dogs, cats should be allowed to bully dogs. Students may become indignant at this assumption, and the hope is that they are able to articulate why such logic is fallacious. In our experience, trials provide many teachable moments, both in real time and during debriefing.

- This exercise is often more challenging for the students than you might suspect. This is one of those lessons where it is important to allow the students to struggle for a while before providing guidance. There is a fine line between challenge and frustration, and it will be up to you to determine whether your students are learning or giving up. Students may be thrown off by the fact that in the first trial, there are no witnesses for the defense. They must use context clues to understand why the provided dialogue is attributable to witnesses for the prosecution, defense lawyers, prosecutors, or the bailiff.

COURT ROLE-PLAY DIALOGUE GUIDE: CASE 1

CASE	DIALOGUE	ROLE	COLOR/ LABEL	NOTES
1	All rise. Court is now in session, the honorable judge (teacher's name) presiding.	Bailiff	Color 1 Label B-1	This is the classic opening for a trial.
1	On the night of August 5, the police were called to the pizza parlor on the corner of Fifth and Front Street known as Sal's. A robbery had taken place at approximately 10:00 pm. Fingerprints taken from the scene matched those of the defendant, Dana Smith.	Prosecution	Color 1 Label P-2	The text outlines the circumstances of the crime and the evidence to be presented against the defendant. Therefore, it is the opening statement by the prosecution.
1	My client, Dana Smith, was sound asleep on the night in question. The police awoke Smith by pounding on the door in the middle of the night. Smith was unaware that a robbery had taken place.	Defense	Color 1 Label D-3	The text outlines the circumstances of the crime and the evidence to be presented in defense of the charge. This is the opening statement by the defense.
1	The prosecution calls Detective Casey Cooper to the stand. (Wait for witness to take the stand.) Do you swear to tell the truth, the whole truth, and nothing but the truth, so help you God?	Bailiff	Color 1 Label P-4	The bailiff calls and swears in the witness.
1	Detective, according to the police log for August 5, you were called to Sal's to investigate a robbery. Can you describe what you found at the scene when you arrived? Did you find any evidence that pointed to a specific suspect?	Prosecution	Color 1 Label P-5	The open-ended questions mark this as direct examination, and the witness is identified as a police officer, usually a witness for the prosecution.

CASE	DIALOGUE	ROLE	COLOR/ LABEL	NOTES
1	Yes, I was called to the scene of the crime on August 5. When I arrived at Sal's, I found the place in chaos. According to the owner, the restaurant had been robbed from the takeout window. The theft was discovered at the end of the evening when the registers were counted. The owner, Sal, accused a regular customer, Dana Smith. We dusted for fingerprints in the takeout window area and were able to match them to those of the defendant.	Witness for the prosecution (detective)	Color 1 Label P-6	The details presented make it clear that this is the testimony of a witness.
1	Detective, you have been on the force a long time, have you not? So you are very familiar with crime scene protocol? Isn't it unusual to stop dusting for fingerprints after lifting only one set?	Defense	Color 1 Label D-7	The specific questioning technique used here is typical of cross-examination. Because we know this is a prosecution witness (the detective), this must be the defense's cross-examination.
1	I have been on the force for 15 years. I wrote the book on crime scene protocol! Well, Sal was very sure about the thief's identity, and when the fingerprints were a match, we thought it was an open-and-shut case.	Witness for the prosecution (detective)	Color 1 Label P-8	The prosecution's witness gives clear answers to the cross-examination questions.
1	The prosecution calls Sal Passano to the stand. (Wait for witness to take the stand.) Do you swear to tell the truth, the whole truth, and nothing but the truth, so help you God?	Bailiff	Color 1 Label P-9	The bailiff calls and swears in the witness.

CASE	DIALOGUE	ROLE	COLOR/LABEL	NOTES
1	How many customers were in your restaurant the night of the robbery? According to the police log, the fingerprints in question were taken from the inside of the takeout window. How many of your customers would have access to that area?	Prosecution	Color 1 Label P-10	The lawyer is asking questions to the restaurant owner, who would be a witness for the prosecution.
1	On the night of the robbery, we had a very busy evening. Everyone wants to eat at Sal's! The takeout window area is restricted to my employees only; there should not have been any customers in that area.	Witness for the prosecution (Sal Passano)	Color 1 Label P-11	This is a clear response to the prosecutor's question.
1	Sal Passano, I understand that you are the owner of Sal's Pizza Parlor and that your restaurant was robbed on the night in question. Do you recognize my client, Dana Smith? Is Dana a regular customer?	Defense	Color 1 Label D-12	The mention of "my client" indicates that this is a cross-examination question from the defense.
1	I certainly do recognize that no-good thief! Dana has the nerve to come into my shop every day for food and then turn around and rob me!	Witness for the prosecution (Sal Passano)	Color 1 Label P-13	This is a clear response to the defense's question.
1	I see—so Dana was in your restaurant almost every day, meaning that the fingerprints gathered could have been made at a time other than the robbery.	Defense	Color 1 Label D-14	This is a cross-examination follow-up to the witness's previous answer, casting doubt on the evidence.
1	Well . . . I don't see how that . . . I *suppose* the fingerprints could have been left at a different time, yes.	Witness for the prosecution (Sal Passano)	Color 1 Label P-15	This is a clear response to the defense's question.

CASE	DIALOGUE	ROLE	COLOR/ LABEL	NOTES
1	My client, Dana Smith, is being charged on the basis of fingerprints that could have been placed at any time prior to the robbery. Surely given that my client is a regular customer, the staff would have recognized a familiar face committing a robbery!	Defense	Color 1 Label D-16	The use of the phrase "my client" marks this as a statement made by the defense, and it wraps up the evidence, marking it as a closing statement.
1	You have heard the police evidence placing the defendant, Dana Smith, at the scene of the crime— indeed, the defendant was the only nonemployee to go behind the counter. Clearly, the defendant is guilty as charged!	Prosecution	Color 1 Label P-17	The charge of guilt marks this as a statement by the prosecution, and the conclusive nature of the language identifies it as a closing statement.

COURT ROLE-PLAY DIALOGUE CARDS: CASE 1

All rise. Court is now in session, the honorable judge (teacher's name) presiding.

On the night of August 5, the police were called to the pizza parlor on the corner of Fifth and Front Street known as Sal's. A robbery had taken place at approximately 10:00 pm. Fingerprints taken from the scene matched those of the defendant, Dana Smith.

My client, Dana Smith, was sound asleep on the night in question. The police awoke Smith by pounding on the door in the middle of the night. Smith was unaware that a robbery had taken place.

The prosecution calls Detective Casey Cooper to the stand. (Wait for witness to take the stand.) Do you swear to tell the truth, the whole truth, and nothing but the truth, so help you God?

Detective, according to the police log for August 5, you were called to Sal's to investigate a robbery. Can you describe what you found at the scene when you arrived? Did you find any evidence that pointed to a specific suspect?

Yes, I was called to the scene of the crime on August 5. When I arrived at Sal's, I found the place in chaos. According to the owner, the restaurant had been robbed from the takeout window. The theft was discovered at the end of the evening when the registers were counted. The owner, Sal, accused a regular customer, Dana Smith. We dusted for fingerprints in the takeout window area and were able to match them to those of the defendant.

Order in the Court © Taylor & Francis Group

Detective, you have been on the force a long time, have you not? So you are very familiar with crime scene protocol? Isn't it unusual to stop dusting for fingerprints after lifting only one set?	I have been on the force for 15 years. I wrote the book on crime scene protocol! Well, Sal was very sure about the thief's identity, and when the fingerprints were a match, we thought it was an open-and-shut case.
The prosecution calls Sal Passano to the stand. (Wait for witness to take the stand.) Do you swear to tell the truth, the whole truth, and nothing but the truth, so help you God?	How many customers were in your restaurant the night of the robbery? According to the police log, the fingerprints in question were taken from the inside of the takeout window. How many of your customers would have access to that area?
On the night of the robbery, we had a very busy evening. Everyone wants to eat at Sal's! The takeout window area is restricted to my employees only; there should not have been any customers in that area.	Sal Passano, I understand that you are the owner of Sal's Pizza Parlor and that your restaurant was robbed on the night in question. Do you recognize my client, Dana Smith? Is Dana a regular customer?
I certainly do recognize that no-good thief! Dana has the nerve to come into my shop every day for food and then turn around and rob me!	I see—so Dana was in your restaurant almost every day, meaning that the fingerprints gathered could have been made at a time other than the robbery.
Well . . . I don't see how that . . . I *suppose* the fingerprints could have been left at a different time, yes.	My client, Dana Smith, is being charged on the basis of fingerprints that could have been placed at any time prior to the robbery. Surely given that my client is a regular customer, the staff would have recognized a familiar face committing a robbery!

You have heard the police evidence placing the defendant, Dana Smith, at the scene of the crime—indeed, the defendant was the only nonemployee to go behind the counter. Clearly, the defendant is guilty as charged!

COURT ROLE-PLAY DIALOGUE
GUIDE: CASE 2

CASE	DIALOGUE	ROLE	COLOR/ LABEL	NOTES
2	All rise. Court is now in session, the honorable judge (teacher's name) presiding.	Bailiff	Color 2 Label B-1	This is the classic opening for a trial.
2	In the case of Fido vs. The Tabby Group, it will be proven beyond a shadow of a doubt that cats are smarter than dogs, and therefore that the tabbies had every right to direct Fido's actions. We will call an expert to the stand who will testify that cats' brains are more responsive than those of dogs.	Prosecutor	Color 2 Label P-2	The text outlines the circumstances of the crime and the evidence to be presented against the defendant. Therefore, it is the opening statement by the prosecution.
2	My client, Fido, has been unfairly harassed by a pack of neighborhood cats. They maintain that cats are smarter than dogs, so they were justified in bossing Fido around. However, we will prove that dogs, having larger brains than cats, are the smarter of the two species. Therefore, Fido was justified in fighting back against these inferior animals.	Defense	Color 2 Label D-3	The text outlines the circumstances of the crime and the evidence to be presented in defense of the charge. This is the opening statement by the defense.
2	The prosecution calls Dr. Thumb to the stand. (Wait for the witness to take the stand.) Do you swear to tell the truth, the whole truth, and nothing but the truth, so help you God?	Bailiff	Color 2 Label B-4	The bailiff calls and swears in the witness.

CASE	DIALOGUE	ROLE	COLOR/ LABEL	NOTES
2	Dr. Thumb, I understand that you are an animal expert. You have done extensive research on whether cats' brains are more responsive than dogs' brains. Could you describe your findings for the court?	Prosecutor	Color 2 Label P-5	The open-ended question marks this as a direct examination.
2	Yes, I am a recognized expert in the field of animal intelligence. My research has proven beyond a shadow of a doubt that cats' brains are indeed more responsive than the slower-witted dogs' brains. We conducted a double-blind study in which we measured the reaction times of different animals in terms of learned behavior when they were rewarded with a treat. The study showed that cats were much faster in their learning processes than dogs.	Witness for the prosecution (Dr. Thumb)	Color 2 Label P-6	The contents of this testimony mark the speaker as a witness for the prosecution.
2	Dr. Thumb, you described your research findings for the court. I have a few questions for you. In your research, you measured response by rewarding the animals with tuna fish treats. The more treats they earned, the more responsive they were. Are cats more attracted to fish than dogs?	Defense	Color 2 Label D-7	The specific questioning technique identifies these questions as cross-examination. Also, we know that Dr. Thumb is a witness for the prosecution. Thus, this is cross-examination by the defense.

CASE	DIALOGUE	ROLE	COLOR/ LABEL	NOTES
2	Well, I hardly think that is relevant to the well-respected research we have accomplished. After all, everyone knows dogs will eat anything. Cats have a much more discerning palate. Therefore, it was necessary to use a reward that would be more attractive to cats.	Witness for the prosecution (Dr. Thumb)	Color 2 Label P-8	The doctor gives a clear response to the cross-examination questions.
2	The Defense calls Dr. Roberts to the stand. (Wait for the witness to take the stand.) Do you swear to tell the truth, the whole truth, and nothing but the truth, so help you God?	Bailiff	Color 2 Label B-9	The bailiff calls and swears in the witness.
2	Dr. Roberts, I understand that you are an animal-intelligence expert who has completed research about the size of cats' brains versus the size of dogs' brains. What did your research show?	Defense	Color 2 Label D-10	The open-ended nature of the question identifies it as a direct examination question.
2	Yes, I am a recognized expert in the field of animal intelligence. In comparing these two similar animal species' brains, we have conclusively proven that dogs, having a larger brain capacity, are capable of far more extensive learning than are cats.	Witness for the defense (Dr. Roberts)	Color 2 Label D-11	This is a clear response to the defense's question.

CASE	DIALOGUE	ROLE	COLOR/LABEL	NOTES
2	Dr. Roberts, you have stated that your research showed that cats' brains are smaller and therefore inferior to dogs' brains. Are elephants' brains larger than humans' brains? Does this make elephants more intelligent than humans?	Prosecution	Color 2 Label P-12	The tone and logic of this question are challenging, marking it as cross-examination by the prosecution.
2	Well, I hardly think that statement is fair. You are greatly simplifying my very intricate research! Cats and dogs have much more in common than do elephants and humans—cats and dogs are comparable, whereas elephants and humans, of course, are incomparable.	Witness for the defense (Dr. Roberts)	Color 2 Label D-13	The witness provides a clear response to the cross-examination question.
2	Fido is a law-abiding dog who was doing nothing wrong when these hostile animals decided to act as a gang of bullies. Is there any wonder that Fido fought back? Should Fido be prosecuted for self-defense? I think not!	Defense	Color 2 Label D-14	The conclusive nature of this dialogue, along with a tone that is sympathetic to the defense, marks this as the closing statement by the defense.
2	Expert witnesses have testified that cats are indeed smarter than dogs, and their actions did not warrant the violent attack by the defendant, who is quite obviously guilty as charged.	Prosecution	Color 2 Label P-15	The charge of guilt and the conclusive language here mark this as the closing statement by the prosecution.

COURT ROLE-PLAY DIALOGUE
CARDS: CASE 2

All rise. Court is now in session, the honorable judge (teacher's name) presiding.	In the case of Fido vs. The Tabby Group, it will be proven beyond a shadow of a doubt that cats are smarter than dogs, and therefore that the tabbies had every right to direct Fido's actions. We will call an expert to the stand who will testify that cats' brains are more responsive than those of dogs.
My client, Fido, has been unfairly harassed by a pack of neighborhood cats. They maintain that cats are smarter than dogs, so they were justified in bossing Fido around. However, we will prove that dogs, having larger brains than cats, are the smarter of the two species. Therefore, Fido was justified in fighting back against these inferior animals.	The prosecution calls Dr. Thumb to the stand. (Wait for the witness to take the stand.) Do you swear to tell the truth, the whole truth, and nothing but the truth, so help you God?
Dr. Thumb, I understand that you are an animal expert. You have done extensive research on whether cats' brains are more responsive than dogs' brains. Could you describe your findings for the court?	Yes, I am a recognized expert in the field of animal intelligence. My research has proven beyond a shadow of a doubt that cats' brains are indeed more responsive than the slower-witted dogs' brains. We conducted a double-blind study in which we measured the reaction times of different animals in terms of learned behavior when they were rewarded with a treat. The study showed that cats were much faster in their learning processes than dogs.

Dr. Thumb, you described your research findings for the court. I have a few questions for you. In your research, you measured response by rewarding the animals with tuna fish treats. The more treats they earned, the more responsive they were. Are cats more attracted to fish than dogs?

Well, I hardly think that is relevant to the well-respected research we have accomplished. After all, everyone knows dogs will eat anything. Cats have a much more discerning palate. Therefore, it was necessary to use a reward that would be more attractive to cats.

The Defense calls Dr. Roberts to the stand. (Wait for the witness to take the stand.) Do you swear to tell the truth, the whole truth, and nothing but the truth, so help you God?

Dr. Roberts, I understand that you are an animal-intelligence expert who has completed research about the size of cats' brains versus the size of dogs' brains. What did your research show?

Yes, I am a recognized expert in the field of animal intelligence. In comparing these two similar animal species' brains, we have conclusively proven that dogs, having a larger brain capacity, are capable of far more extensive learning than are cats.

Dr. Roberts, you have stated that your research showed that cats' brains are smaller and therefore inferior to dogs' brains. Are elephants' brains larger than humans' brains? Does this make elephants more intelligent than humans?

Well, I hardly think that statement is fair. You are greatly simplifying my very intricate research! Cats and dogs have much more in common than do elephants and humans—cats and dogs are comparable, whereas elephants and humans, of course, are incomparable.

Fido is a law-abiding dog who was doing nothing wrong when these hostile animals decided to act as a gang of bullies. Is there any wonder that Fido fought back? Should Fido be prosecuted for self-defense? I think not!

Expert witnesses have testified that cats are indeed smarter than dogs, and their actions did not warrant the violent attack by the defendant, who is quite obviously guilty as charged.

Lesson 3

Concepts

- Court procedure
- Trial sequence
- Objections
- Terms from Lessons 1 and 2

Materials

- Roles and Duties of Court Personnel sheet (p. 43)
- Phases of Court Proceedings sheet (p. 45)
- Rules of Evidence sheet (p. 46)
- Standard Objections sheet (p. 47)
- Role Assignments sheet (p. 48)
- Instructions for Bailiff/Presiding Juror packet (pp. 49–51)
- Instructions for Witnesses packet (pp. 52–56)
- Instructions for Prosecuting Attorneys packet (pp. 57–63)
- Instructions for Defense Attorneys packet (pp. 64–70)
- Jon Scieszka's *The True Story of the Big Bad Wolf*

Student Objective

The student demonstrates an understanding of the roles in a courtroom and the sequence of a trial by applying those terms to a familiar case based on a fairy tale.

Introduction

First, read or tell the traditional version of "The Three Little Pigs." If you do not have a book version of this, we have provided a narrative on page 53. Next, read Jon Scieszka's *The True Story of the Big Bad Wolf.*

DOI: 10.4324/9781003236955-7

Recognition

Students, using the vocabulary words introduced in the two previous lessons, identify the roles that the characters in the story would take on in a courtroom (e.g., the wolf would be the defendant) and discuss the implications of this.

Application

In small groups, students move through the material.

1. Students read and highlight the general handout and the Standard Objections sheet.
2. Students work with the teacher, who distributes the papers corresponding to specific roles.
3. The students ask any questions they may have.

Problem Solving

Students prepare for the trial.

1. Students should assume their roles as identified on their Role Assignments sheets.
2. Using what they have learned about courtroom procedures, students should understand what will be expected of their characters and prepare accordingly.

Grade-Level Expectations

The student:

- Shows breadth of vocabulary knowledge, demonstrating understanding of word meanings or relationships by the use of words in context.
- Demonstrates initial understanding of informational text by organizing information to show understanding.
- Uses comprehension strategies before, during, and after reading informational texts.

Additional Notes

- This is where the fun really begins! This section is designed to allow students to enact the courtroom roles they have learned about using a case they are quite familiar with—that of the popular fairy tale "The Three Little Pigs."
- We have provided copies of "The Three Little Pigs" and "Little Red Riding Hood" for you to share with students, some of whom will be unfamiliar with the stories. (Little Red Riding Hood serves in this trial as a character witness for the wolf.) You can also improvise and tell the stories aloud, or you could use picture book versions. However, it is important that whatever materials you use do not contradict one another, and further, that they allow students

to have a trial. For example, in some versions of "The Three Little Pigs," the first two pigs escape, and in most versions of "Little Red Riding Hood," the wolf is killed at the end—these versions would not be very helpful!

- Whichever versions of the stories you use, the witnesses and lawyers will have to use those versions as the facts of the case, from which they may not deviate (although evidence and testimony that aligns with the facts of the case can be created). In other words, the witnesses' testimonies during the trial should not deviate from the letters they write to the judge, which in turn should be aligned with whatever versions of the stories you use, as should the lawyers' questions and evidence. We have numbered the witness sheets for clarity, but the defense and the prosecution can call witnesses in whatever order they choose.

- In terms of casting roles for the trial, keep in mind that the bailiff controls the order of the trial, but does not have to think on his or her feet very much; thus, this may be a good role for a student who is struggling. The witnesses (this includes the plaintiff and the defendant) are only in charge of knowing their own stories, making witness roles suitable for students who are in the middle. The lawyer roles are the most complicated—lawyers are the ones who must synthesize information and think on their feet. We sometimes opt to save the highest ability students for lawyer roles in the next trial (see Lesson 6), which is more demanding. Clearly, this trial format works well with a heterogeneous group. However, it is certainly suitable for a homogenous group as well, particularly for use with high-ability students. Discussing the trial afterwards, and allowing all students to participate and comment, will give students in the roles with less flexibility a chance to demonstrate analytical skills.

- This trial will present challenges for the students as they get their footing and deal with the context in a real-time setting. Sometimes it is helpful to have students conduct a dry run, where they move through an abbreviated outline of the order of the proceedings before Lesson 4. It may be necessary to help students if they falter, but try to let them figure things out on their own!

- The prosecution is responsible for posting the charges they intend to bring against the defendant during the preparation phase. (We have had them post the charges on the blackboard.) This way, the defense is aware of what it must do to avoid a guilty verdict. Remind the prosecution lawyers that they must prove beyond question the guilt of the defendant. It may be better to use a lesser charge and prove it than to try for the highest crime possible and fall short. For example, if students can prove that the wolf killed the first two pigs—but they cannot prove that he planned it—then the charge should be murder in the second degree. You can discuss charges and burdens of proof if you wish to augment the lesson, or you can simplify things by allowing students to state their charges more simply.

- Use your judgment when it comes to guiding students as they read through and digest the information packet. You may need to discuss and reinforce some ideas.
- Make sure that students understand how to examine witnesses. They should be able to distinguish between open-ended questioning, in which witnesses are allowed to elaborate and tell their stories, and cross-examination, in which witnesses are asked direct questions and must answer with only the information asked of them. We do not give lawyers the opportunity to redirect after their side's witnesses are cross-examined. We have found that generally this lengthens the trial too much; limiting the witness examination to direct and cross examination is usually suitable for students' attention spans. Rather, if the lawyers wish to address something that was said during cross-examination, they can incorporate it into their closing statement.
- Likewise, the witnesses need to know that their mission is to tell their side of the story whenever they can. Lawyers can practice with their own witnesses, but they should not be in contact with the other side's witnesses until they meet them on the stand.
- We have not found it necessary to implement time limits on the opening and closing statements, but you may find that limiting students to 3 minutes is useful. If anything, we find that students' statements are usually too short, but if you wish, you can discuss time limits with students before they begin their preparations.
- Students can elaborate on their stories as long as they do not change the facts. It is also admissible to manufacture evidence. We have had students produce fingerprint evidence! Other students have used the pictures in Jon Scieszka's book as photographic evidence. Encourage students to be creative—the point is for them to make connections between the evidence and the points they are trying to prove. Many students in our classes have asked if they can wear costume pieces or bring in props for the trial. We have encouraged this in order to foster student engagement, but be careful that the props and costumes do not become more important than students' preparation for the trial!
- When lawyers are organizing their questions, they should consider the points they wish to bring out in the testimony and *then* write their questions.
- Sheets are provided to help the bailiff organize the necessary information. The bailiff should also serve as the presiding juror when his or her team is on the jury. In the bailiff's instructions, he or she is told to make a list of 10 guiding questions to ask the jury members in order to guide the conversation during deliberation. This helps augment the bailiff role, which would otherwise be very small.

Roles and Duties of Court Personnel

Bailiff

This officer of the court opens the trial by calling the court to order and announcing the judge. It is customary for everyone in the court to rise as the judge enters as a gesture of respect for the law. The bailiff keeps the trial running according to the established routine and escorts witnesses to the witness stand. The bailiff is responsible for the swearing in of witnesses by saying, "Do you swear to tell the truth, the whole truth, and nothing but the truth, so help you God?" Witnesses are required to place their left hands on the bible and raise their right hands as the bailiff asks this question. The appropriate response is "I do." As an officer of the court, the bailiff is also expected to keep order during the trial. The bailiff will act as the presiding juror when his or her team is acting as the jury. Thus, there are two bailiffs, one for each trial.

Prosecuting Attorney(s)

The prosecution may include one or more lawyers who are responsible for arguing the plaintiff's case. They must present the case according to the facts and provide evidence of the defendant's guilt. This evidence is provided by both eyewitnesses and expert witnesses. Sometimes physical evidence is available to be presented to the court as exhibits. The lawyers for the prosecution make an **opening statement** of the facts of the case from their point of view, conduct a **direct examination** of the witnesses that supports their point of view, conduct a **cross-examination** of the witnesses from the defense to try to discredit their stories, and end by summarizing their case in the **closing argument**.

Defense Attorney(s)

The defense must argue the case from the defendant's point of view. They must present the case according to the facts and provide evidence of the defendant's innocence. This evidence is provided by both eyewitnesses and expert witnesses. Sometimes physical evidence is available, to be presented to the court as exhibits. The lawyers for the defense make an **opening statement** of the facts of the case from their point of view, conduct a **direct examination** of the witnesses that supports their point of view, conduct a **cross-examination** of the witnesses from the defense to try to discredit their stories, and end by summarizing their case in the **closing argument**.

Plaintiff

The plaintiff is the accuser—the person who is bringing the suit against the defendant. This person is represented by the prosecution and will be called to testify as a witness.

Defendant

The defendant is the person being accused of wrongdoing. He or she is represented by the defense and will be called as a witness.

Witnesses

These are people who have eyewitness accounts to share regarding the facts of the case. They may also be people who the court views as experts (at the judge's discretion) in the area in which they will be questioned. For example, a medical doctor could be an expert witness in the effects of certain illnesses. Witnesses may only answer questions that pertain to the case. Witnesses are called by either the prosecution or the defense. If the defense or the prosecution calls a specific witness, they may interview that witness before the trial begins. This allows lawyers and witnesses to practice the direct examination phase of the witnesses' testimony. However, a witness should never discuss the case with the opposing lawyers, except during cross-examination.

Jury

The jury is usually made up of 12 people who have no connection to the participants in the case. They listen carefully to the trial without discussing it among themselves. When the trial is over, the jury members discuss the information that has been presented and try to come to a unanimous decision as to the defendant's guilt or innocence. This must be based *solely* on the evidence they have heard in the court! The **presiding juror** is in charge of posing questions to the group to encourage discussion. The presiding juror must also present the jury's decision to the judge.

Phases of Court Proceedings

Opening Statement

The prosecution and the defense each must make an opening statement describing the facts of the case from its client's point of view. This is simply an opportunity to state the facts and to tell the jury how those facts will be proved. It is not time to produce actual evidence. For example, the defense may say, "We will provide evidence that our client was not at the scene of the crime."

Direct Examination

Each side will have the opportunity to call its witnesses one by one to the stand. The lawyers must be careful about the type of questions they ask. The object is to allow the witness to tell his or her story, but the questions must ask the witness for specific information. Specific questions that are also pertinent and will allow witnesses to explain themselves are those such as "Where were you on the night in question?" and "What did you see at the henhouse that night?" Asking, "What do you know about this case?" is too broad a question to ask. Witnesses may only be asked about their relevant experiences and, in the case of an expert witness, information about which they are experts.

Cross-Examination

Any witness called to the stand for direct examination may be cross-examined by the opposing side. The purpose is for the opposing team to try to redirect questioning in such a way as to cast doubt on the witness's story. For example, a defense lawyer who is cross-examining one of the prosecution's witnesses may say, "We have just heard you identify my client as the person you saw on the night in question. However, I see that you are wearing glasses. Are you in the habit of removing your glasses before you go to bed? How can you be sure that the person you saw was my client, given that you were some distance away from that person and were not wearing your glasses? In order to be successful in cross-examination, lawyers must listen very carefully to the witnesses' answers during their direct examination.

Closing Statement

Each side in the case is given the opportunity to summarize its findings at the end of the trial. It is important to restate the strong points that held up during direct examination and any doubts successfully created during cross-examination. It is also important for each team to cast its client in a positive light, either as the wronged party or as the wrongfully accused party.

Rules of Evidence

There are six types of questions that may be objected to by the opposing attorneys.

1. **Hearsay.** An objection can be made to a witness's statement that is offered to prove a fact, but that the witness was not actually present to hear. For example, if a witness says, "I have heard people say that Mr. Smith hates cats," then the witness did not ever actually hear Mr. Smith say that he hated cats.

2. **Irrelevant evidence.** Witnesses may be asked only about facts that are directly about the case itself. For instance, if a witness were asked his or her age, then the opposing team could object, saying that the witness's age had no direct connection to the case.

3. **Lack of personal knowledge.** Witnesses may not be asked questions about the facts of the case of which they have no personal knowledge. For instance, "Do you think Mr. Smith hated cats?" would constitute lack of personal knowledge, as the witness would merely be making an opinion, rather than stating a known fact.

4. **Leading questions.** This rule of evidence applies only to direct examination questions. A leading question suggests to the witness the answer that is desired by the examiner. It is often worded so that the witness can give a simple yes or no answer (e.g., "You are not a very good judge of character, are you, Mr. Smith?").

5. **Opinion.** A witness must not be asked for his or her opinion at any time. The witness may only be asked to testify as to the facts of a case by describing something he or she saw or a relevant conversation. An examiner may not ask a witness to give his or her opinion of a situation(e.g., "What do you think Mr. Smith intended to do?").

6. **Argumentative question.** A lawyer may not ask the same question over and over again in attempts to get the witness to give a different answer than the one already given.

STANDARD OBJECTIONS

WHO MAY OBJECT

LAWYERS

WHAT THEY MAY OBJECT TO

1. DIRECT EXAMINATION BY OPPONENT
2. CROSS-EXAMINATION BY OPPONENT
3. WITNESSES' ANSWERS

WHAT THEY MAY NOT OBJECT TO

OPENING STATEMENT   CLOSING ARGUMENT

REASONS THEY MAY OBJECT

IRRELEVANT EVIDENCE	LACK OF PERSONAL KNOWLEDGE	LEADING QUESTION
The evidence has no connection with the focus of the case.	The witness is asked to speculate on something about which he or she has no direct knowledge.	A question is asked that suggests the answer to the witness.
HEARSAY	ARGUMENTATIVE QUESTION	OPINION
The witness provides evidence based on rumors or information from someone else.	The lawyer badgers the witness with repeated questions, hoping for a different answer.	Only expert witnesses may be asked to give their opinions.

Name:_____ Date: _____

ROLE ASSIGNMENTS

ROLE	TEAM A	TEAM B
Bailiff/Presiding Juror		
PROSECUTION		
Ms. Petunia Pig, Plaintiff		
Prosecuting Attorney #1		
Prosecuting Attorney #2		
Little Red Riding Hood, Witness		
DEFENSE		
Mr. B. B. Wolf, Defendant		
Defense Attorney # 1		
Defense Attorney #2		
Dr. Wolfgang, Witness		

Order in the Court © Taylor & Francis Group

Instructions for Bailiff/Presiding Juror

When your team is the one participating in the trial, you will act as bailiff. During this time, it is your job to call up the appropriate people when it is their turn to speak. In addition, you will keep the trial flowing smoothly. When your team makes up the jury, you will play the role of presiding juror, meaning that you will be the jury's spokesperson. You should make a list of 10 questions about the case to ask the jury when you are deliberating about the case; these questions will guide the conversation.

In order to be successful in your job, ask the two teams which students are playing which role, and fill in the Trial Roles sheet. In addition, work with the defense and prosecution of your team to fill out the Order of Trial sheet with the names of the various participants and who is responsible for each part of the trial.

Name:_____ Date: _____

TRIAL ROLES

JUDGE: _____

PLAINTIFF: _____

DEFENDANT: _____

PROSECUTING ATTORNEYS:

1. _____

2. _____

DEFENSE ATTORNEYS:

1. _____

2. _____

WITNESSES FOR THE PROSECUTION:

1. _____

2. _____

WITNESSES FOR THE DEFENSE:

1. _____

2. _____

Order in the Court © Taylor & Francis Group

ORDER OF TRIAL

1. CALL COURT TO ORDER

   Bailiff

2. OPENING STATEMENTS

   a. Prosecution: _____

   b. Defense: _____

3. FIRST WITNESS FOR THE PROSECUTION:

   a. Direct Examination: _____

   b. Cross-Examination: _____

4. SECOND WITNESS FOR THE PROSECUTION:

   a. Direct Examination: _____

   b. Cross-Examination: _____

5. FIRST WITNESS FOR THE DEFENSE:

   a. Direct Examination: _____

   b. Cross-Examination: _____

6. SECOND WITNESS FOR THE DEFENSE:

   a. Direct Examination: _____

   b. Cross-Examination: _____

7. CLOSING ARGUMENTS

   a. Defense: _____

   b. Prosecution: _____

Instructions for Witnesses

After reviewing the facts of the case, you must write a letter to the judge presenting your side of the case. This letter may make the difference in whether the judge rules in your favor!

It is important that you express your strong feelings about this case. Remember, you are trying to persuade someone to take your side. It is important to be respectful, use appropriate language, and make sure the letter looks polished and is carefully written. Making a good impression is extremely useful in persuading someone of something.

For example, if you are charged with running a stop sign, but it is because you were unable to see the sign, you might write:

> I am very sorry that I ran a stop sign; my driving record has been excellent up to this point. I feel it is only fair to report that the sign in question is completely covered by weeds and is not visible from the street. Moreover, the police officer was in his car, which was hidden behind the weeds as well; he was waiting for a driver to miss the sign.

Rather than:

> That cop was just waiting to nab me! It's not fair! He covered the sign and set me up! You would be really stupid to make me pay this fine!

It is also very important that you not lie in your witness statement. You must go off of the facts of the case, although you may include information that was not presented if it aligns with the facts. When you testify in the trial, you will need to give testimony that is aligned with what you write in your letter.

Write a rough draft, and then revise it and address a final copy to the judge. Don't forget to sign your name!

THE FACTS OF THE CASE: THE TALE OF THE THREE LITTLE PIGS

Once upon a time, there lived at the edge of the woods a large family of pigs. One day, Mama and Papa Pig sat down together and discussed the problem of space in their small home. They decided it was time for their three oldest children to make homes of their own. They called the three pigs together and said, "Pete, Pat, and Petunia, you are our pride and joy! We have watched you grow and tried to teach you to work hard and do the right thing. It is time for you to go out into the world and make a life for yourselves." The three pigs were excited but nervous about going into the woods alone. They packed their few belongings and said goodbye to their family. Mr. and Mrs. Pig gave them one last piece of advice: "Beware of the Big Bad Wolf in the woods. He is very dangerous!" The three pigs assured their parents that they would be careful and went skipping down the trail toward their new lives.

The first and oldest little pig was named Pete. He was a happy little pig who loved to play the fiddle. Pete was not especially fond of hard work. As they walked down the path, Pete spied a pile of straw. "Aha!" Pete said. "This straw is perfect for the house I am going to build!" He gathered up the straw and quick as a wink, he threw together a house of straw. The other little pigs continued down the trail listening to Pete's happy fiddle playing.

The second little pig was named Pat. Pat was also not a fan of hard work but realized there was some merit in it. Pat thought Pete was being very foolish to build such a shoddy house as one made of straw. Pat spied a pile of wood further down the path and quickly claimed it for his own. The third little pig tried to convince him that wood was little better than the straw, but Pat was sure that a wooden house would be much safer. Pat spent about a day building the wooden house and then settled in for a good nap.

Meanwhile the third and youngest little pig, Petunia, continued down the trail. Petunia knew the value of hard work and had taken her parents' advice about the Big Bad Wolf very seriously. When she found a large pile of bricks, she decided that this was the perfect material for her house. She labored day and night for a whole week. Her siblings were very impatient with her. Pete said, "Your pounding is drowning out my fiddle playing!" Pat said," Your pounding is disturbing my nap!" But Petunia kept at her job until she had built the strongest house she could.

No sooner had she finished her house than there came a knock on Pete's straw house door. It was the Big Bad Wolf! "Little pig, little pig, let me in," said the wolf.

Pete answered, "Not by the hair on my chinny chin chin!"

The wolf said, "Then I'll huff and I'll puff and I'll blow your house down!" And he huffed and he puffed and he blew the house down. Pete's fiddle playing was never heard again!

The Big Bad Wolf continued to the next little pig's house. Pat heard him coming and quickly shut and locked his wooden door. "Little pig, little pig, let me in," said the wolf.

Pat answered, "Not by the hair on my chinny chin chin!"

The wolf said, "Then I'll huff and I'll puff and I'll blow your house down!" And he huffed and he puffed and he huffed and he puffed and he blew the house down. Pat was never seen again!

The Big Bad Wolf continued down the trail and came to the brick house of Ms. Petunia Pig. Petunia was safely locked inside her strong brick house. The wolf knocked on the door, "Little pig, little pig, let me in."

Petunia answered, "Not by the hair on my chinny chin chin!"

The wolf said, "Then I'll huff and I'll puff and I'll blow your house down!" And he huffed and he puffed and he huffed and he puffed and he huffed and he puffed but he couldn't blow the house down. The wolf was furious and flew into a rage. Just then, the Forest Patrol arrived and arrested the wolf for his evil deeds!

Order in the Court © Taylor & Francis Group

THE FACTS OF THE CASE: THE TALE OF LITTLE RED RIDING HOOD

Once upon a time, a small family lived at the edge of the woods. The family included a mother, a father, and their little girl. The father was a woodsman who worked hard in the woods all day long. The mother was a famous baker and worked hard to supply the town with her goodies. The little girl played happily in the shadows of the trees. On the other side of the woods lived the mother's mother, the little girl's grandmother. The grandmother had been a seamstress all her life and could make beautiful clothes. In fact, she had made her granddaughter a bright red hooded cape, and all through the region the little girl was now known as Little Red Riding Hood.

One day, after the woodsman had left for work, the mother told Little Red Riding Hood that Grandma was not feeling well. The mother had too much work to do that day to make the journey through the woods to Grandma's house. She asked Little Red if she felt comfortable enough to make the journey alone. Little Red was very excited because this was the first time her mother had entrusted her to walk through the woods alone! After packing a basket full of goodies for Grandma and putting on her red cloak, Little Red was ready. Her mother reminded her not to talk to strangers, and off Little Red went, skipping down the path into the woods.

Little Red had taken the path through the woods many times with her mother and father, so she was not worried about finding her way. She stopped to look at the beautiful flowers and listen to the birdsong along the way. When she had gotten about halfway through the forest, she stopped to rest for a moment under the shade of the old oak tree that grew in the very center of the forest. As she sat and rested she heard another creature approaching.

Unbeknownst to Little Red, she had been being watched carefully as she skipped though the forest. The Big Bad Wolf was tracking the girl and was very interested in what she had in her basket. He came up the side path by the oak tree whistling a happy tune. "Why, it's Little Red Riding Hood," the wolf said as he neared the tree. "Those goodies in your basket smell awfully good!"

Little Red Riding Hood, remembering what her mother had told her about strangers, immediately replied, "I cannot talk to you because I am not allowed to talk to strangers."

The wolf laughed his best carefree laugh and said, "Oh, don't be silly. I am not a stranger! Why, I have known your parents for years! I remember the day you were born."

"Well, in that case," said Little Red Riding Hood, "I suppose I could share a biscuit with you, but I mustn't give you any more than one. These are for my Grandma, who lives on the other side of the woods."

The wolf gobbled down his biscuit, thanked Little Red, and told her to be careful as she finished her journey. "There are many creatures in the woods that would love to gobble you up as I gobbled up your mother's biscuit!" Little Red was uncomfortable with the wolf and happily left him to complete her walk to her grandmother's house.

As soon as she was out of sight, the wolf set off through the woods and took the shortcut to the old woman's cottage. Wasting no time, he walked right in and shut Grandma up in the closet. The wolf quickly put on one of Grandma's nightgowns and sleeping bonnets and got into her bed. He was just pulling the covers up to his large nose when he heard Little Red come into the house.

Little Red called out, "Hello, Grandma, I have brought you some goodies from my mother's kitchen. May I come in?"

In a high-pitched voice, the wolf called, "Why, of course, my dear!"

Little Red came into the bedroom and approached the bed. She looked down and said, "Why, Grandma! What big eyes you have."

The wolf replied, "The better to see you with, my dear."

"Why, Grandma," said Little Red. "What big ears you have!"

"The better to hear you with, my dear," said the wolf.

With a growing sense of alarm, Little Red said, "Why, Grandma! What big teeth you have!"

"The better to eat you with, my dear!" the wolf yelled, and he leapt from the bed and chased Little Red around the house. Little Red's screams reached her father's ears where he was working nearby. He came running just in time to save Little Red, and then he chased the wolf off into the woods.

Father and daughter quickly freed Grandma from the closet. The woodsman was relieved that both Grandma and Little Red were all right. Grandma was furious with the wolf for stealing her nightgown, and Little Red promised never to talk to strangers again!

Instructions for Prosecuting Attorneys

As a member of the prosecution team, you have the job of proving beyond a shadow of a doubt that B. B. Wolf is guilty of the charges filed. It is crucial that you establish a timeline of events and provide evidence to prove your points.

The prosecution team is responsible for preparing the following components of the trial:

- the **opening statement;**
- the **direct examination** of witnesses (you have two witnesses to rely on, Little Red Riding Hood and Petunia Pig);
- the **cross-examination** of witnesses (you have the opportunity to cross-examine the defense's two witnesses, B. B. Wolf and Dr. Wolfgang); and
- the **closing statement.**

Meet as a team and divide up the labor to make the most of your time. For the safety of the community, it is very important that you are successful in putting this dangerous character behind bars!

OPENING STATEMENT: PROSECUTION

Case Title: *Ms. Petunia Pig v. Mr. B. B. Wolf*
Attorney Presenting:

IMPORTANT POINTS

_____

_____

_____

_____

_____

_____

_____

_____

_____

_____

_____

_____

_____

_____

_____

_____

_____

_____

_____

DIRECT EXAMINATION OF
WITNESS #1: PROSECUTION

Case Title: *Ms. Petunia Pig v. Mr. B. B. Wolf*
Attorney Presenting:
Witness: Little Red Riding Hood

Questions:	Important Points
1. _____ _____ _____	
2. _____ _____ _____	
3. _____ _____ _____	
4. _____ _____ _____	
5. _____ _____ _____	

DIRECT EXAMINATION OF
WITNESS #2: PROSECUTION

Case Title: *Ms. Petunia Pig v. Mr. B. B. Wolf*
Attorney Presenting:
Witness: Petunia Pig

Questions:	Important Points
1. _____ _____ _____	
2. _____ _____ _____	
3. _____ _____ _____	
4. _____ _____ _____	
5. _____ _____ _____	

Name:_____ Date: _____

CROSS-EXAMINATION OF
WITNESS #3: PROSECUTION

Case Title: *Ms. Petunia Pig v. Mr. B. B. Wolf*
Attorney Presenting:
Witness: B. B. Wolf

Questions*:	Important Points
1. _____ _____ _____	
2. _____ _____ _____	
3. _____ _____ _____	
4. _____ _____ _____	
5. _____ _____ _____	

*Additional questions based on direct examination testimony and the witness's responses to the above questions may be added during the trial.

Name:_____ Date: _____

CROSS-EXAMINATION OF
WITNESS #4: PROSECUTION

....

Case Title: *Ms. Petunia Pig v. Mr. B. B. Wolf*
Attorney Presenting:
Witness: Dr. Wolfgang

Questions*:	Important Points
1. _____ _____ _____	
2. _____ _____ _____	
3. _____ _____ _____	
4. _____ _____ _____	
5. _____ _____ _____	

*Additional questions based on direct examination testimony and the witness's responses to the above questions may be added during the trial.

Order in the Court © Taylor & Francis Group

Name:_____ Date: _____

CLOSING STATEMENT: PROSECUTION

Case Title: *Ms. Petunia Pig v. Mr. B. B. Wolf*
Attorney Presenting:

IMPORTANT POINTS

_____

_____

_____

_____

_____

_____

_____

_____

_____

_____

_____

_____

_____

_____

_____

_____

_____

_____

Name:_____ Date: _____

Instructions for Defense Attorneys

As a member of the defense team, it is your job to show reasonable doubt that the wolf is guilty of the charges filed. It is crucial that you show the wolf as a poor misunderstood creature being judged unfairly. The pigs' tragic deaths were accidents, and the wolf was merely following his carnivorous nature when he ate the pigs. He certainly did not set out to kill those innocent porkers.

The defense team is responsible for preparing the following components of the trial:

- the **opening statement;**
- the **direct examination** of witnesses (you have two witnesses to rely on, Dr. Wolfgang and B. B. Wolf);
- the **cross-examination** of witnesses (you have the opportunity to cross-examine the prosecution's two witnesses, Petunia Pig and Little Red Riding Hood); and
- the **closing statement.**

Meet as a team and divide up the labor to make the most of your time. In the interest of justice, it is essential that you prove the innocence of this poor wolf!

Name:_____ Date: _____

OPENING STATEMENT: DEFENSE

Case Title: *Ms. Petunia Pig v. Mr. B. B. Wolf*
Attorney Presenting:

IMPORTANT POINTS

_____

_____

_____

_____

_____

_____

_____

_____

_____

_____

_____

_____

_____

_____

_____

_____

_____

CROSS-EXAMINATION OF
WITNESS #1: DEFENSE

Case Title: *Ms. Petunia Pig v. Mr. B. B. Wolf*
Attorney Presenting:
Witness: Little Red Riding Hood

Questions*:	Important Points
1. _____ _____ _____ 2. _____ _____ _____ 3. _____ _____ _____ 4. _____ _____ _____ 5. _____ _____ _____	

*Additional questions based on direct examination testimony and the witness's responses to the above questions may be added during the trial.

CROSS-EXAMINATION OF WITNESS #2: DEFENSE

Case Title: *Ms. Petunia Pig v. Mr. B. B. Wolf*
Attorney Presenting:
Witness: Petunia Pig

Questions*:	Important Points
1. _____ _____ _____ 2. _____ _____ _____ 3. _____ _____ _____ 4. _____ _____ _____ 5. _____ _____ _____	

*Additional questions based on direct examination testimony and the witness's responses to the above questions may be added during the trial.

DIRECT EXAMINATION OF
WITNESS #3: DEFENSE

Case Title: *Ms. Petunia Pig v. Mr. B. B. Wolf*
Attorney Presenting:
Witness: Dr. Wolfgang

Questions:	Important Points
1. _____ _____ _____	
2. _____ _____ _____	
3. _____ _____ _____	
4. _____ _____ _____	
5. _____ _____ _____	

Name:_____ Date: _____

DIRECT EXAMINATION OF
WITNESS #4: DEFENSE

Case Title: *Ms. Petunia Pig v. Mr. B. B. Wolf*
Attorney Presenting:
Witness: B. B. Wolf

Questions:	Important Points
1. _____ _____ _____	
2. _____ _____ _____	
3. _____ _____ _____	
4. _____ _____ _____	
5. _____ _____ _____	

Name:_____ Date: _____

CLOSING STATEMENT: DEFENSE

Case Title: *Ms. Petunia Pig v. Mr. B. B. Wolf*
Attorney Presenting:

IMPORTANT POINTS

_____

_____

_____

_____

_____

_____

_____

_____

_____

_____

_____

_____

_____

_____

_____

_____

Order in the Court © Taylor & Francis Group

Lesson 4

Concepts

- Role of jury members
- Listening skills
- Improvisation based on new information

Materials

- Order of Trial Teacher's Guide sheet (pp. 74–75)
- General rubric (p. 76)
- Role-specific rubrics (pp. 77–79)

Student Objective:

The student demonstrates knowledge of the roles and sequences of a court case by participating in a fairy tale-based trial. Students are able to see the process from both sides by playing courtroom roles and acting as jury members.

Introduction

Students are given 5 minutes to organize themselves for the trial. During this time, the teacher prepares the team that will act as the jury first by instructing them to consider only evidence that is actually presented during the course of the trial, as opposed to relying on prior assumptions or knowledge, which must be disregarded.

Recognition

Jury members put away all of their materials. They may, however, take notes during the trial, so they may keep notebooks and writing utensils out on their desks.

DOI: 10.4324/9781003236955-8

Application

The students run the trial.

1. One team enacts their courtroom roles, and the other team acts as the jury.
2. The teacher or another adult acts as the judge.
3. The students run the case according to the sequence provided in the Order of Trial Teacher's Guide sheet.

Problem Solving

The jury reaches its verdict.

1. The jury deliberates in full view of the other team.
2. The team whose members enacted the courtroom roles may not comment during the jury's discussions.
3. If you wish, you can debrief with both teams, either separately or as a large group, after the presiding juror has delivered the decision.

Grade-Level Expectations

The student:

- Shows breadth of vocabulary knowledge, demonstrating understanding of word meanings or relationships by the use of words in context.
- Demonstrates initial understanding of informational texts by organizing information to show understanding.
- Uses comprehension strategies before, during, and after reading informational texts.

Additional Notes

- We have provided materials to illustrate the order in which the trial should be conducted, but we have not included a specific script to be followed (e.g., "All rise, hear ye, hear ye"). You may make the proceedings more formal by incorporating such a script (easily found online), or you can always prod students or step in and guide them in creating a script.
- Likewise, it is up to you whether there should be a specific procedure that students must stick to when it comes to submitting evidence. Although we require that students obtain teacher approval of the evidence they submit, we do not require them to notify the opposing team or follow a line-by-line script. If you think that students would benefit from a more structured approach—for instance, one in which students had to request permission to approach the witness, produce marked evidence, give it to the judge, and so on—then you can create one.
- Remind the students before the trial that if they get confused during the trial, they may ask to "approach the bench," meaning that they can come up and ask you questions while breaking character. When this occurs, be sure

Lesson 4

that representatives from both the prosecuting team and the defending team hear what you say so that both teams have the same information.

- Watching students make objections is perhaps the most entertaining part of the whole experience. Be sure to review the Standard Objections sheet with the class before the trial. Remember that as the judge, you must make the ruling. Students have to give you reasons to back up their objections!
- You will fill out rubrics as the court is in session. Be sure to have a rubric out for each individual in addition to the general rubric. Use a highlighter to mark the appropriate boxes of the rubrics as the trial progresses, using whatever strategy works best for you. (We usually mark either the left side of the box to indicate that the lowest number of points should be earned, the right side to indicate that the highest number of points should be earned, or the middle to indicate that the average number of points should be earned.)
- On the rubrics, we have not included point ranges. This way, you can decide on a total number of points that you want students to earn and divide up the points accordingly, also incorporating the weight you want to lend to each category. We generally use a fairly narrow range for less important skills and a broader range for those skills that we are emphasizing (or those skills that are more important). This not only imparts to students that certain skills are more valuable than others, but it also functions to make total overall failure less probable, given that there are a few categories in which even a substandard performance will not earn many fewer points than a standard performance. Given that there are seven categories between the two rubrics, an example of point ranges we have used is 0–7 points, 8–11 points, and 12–14 points.
- We have included an Order of Trial Teacher's Guide sheet that you can use as an outline to take notes throughout the trial.
- Having the members of the jury deliberate in front of the courtroom players allows them to share their reasoning. Generally, we ask each jury member to share his or her viewpoints and final vote. This serves not only to underscore the need for discussion and unanimity, but also to encourage contribution from students who are typically more reticent.
- In this trial and the one in Lesson 6, we have found that the students are very focused on who wins and who loses the trials. Sometimes there is a clear winning side, but often there is no victor. It is important to stress that whether or not students win the trial does not determine their grades. Rather, their grades are determined by how well they play their roles and back up their cases with evidence. Because students can tend to get slightly emotional about winning or losing cases, however, it is important to debrief at the close of the period to avoid finger pointing among students regarding whose fault a lost trial was. Be sure to tune in to students' reactions in order to avert potential issues.

ORDER OF TRIAL TEACHER'S GUIDE

1. CALL COURT TO ORDER
   Bailiff

   _____

   _____

2. OPENING STATEMENTS
   a. Prosecution:_____

   _____

   _____

   b. Defense: _____

   _____

   _____

3. FIRST WITNESS FOR THE PROSECUTION:_____

   a. Direct Examination: _____

   _____

   _____

   b. Cross-Examination: _____

   _____

   _____

4. SECOND WITNESS FOR THE PROSECUTION: _____

   a. Direct Examination: _____

   _____

   _____

   b. Cross-Examination: _____

   _____

   _____

5. FIRST WITNESS FOR THE DEFENSE:_____

    a. Direct Examination: _____

    _____

    _____

    b. Cross-Examination: _____

    _____

    _____

6. SECOND WITNESS FOR THE DEFENSE:_____

    a. Direct Examination: _____

    _____

    _____

    b. Cross-Examination: _____

    _____

    _____

7. CLOSING ARGUMENTS

    a. Defense: _____

    _____

    _____

    b. Prosecution: _____

    _____

    _____

GENERAL RUBRIC

	Excellent	Good	Needs Work
Authentic Role-Playing	You displayed an understanding of courtroom roles by staying within the limits of your character and even adding personal touches.	You displayed a basic understanding of courtroom roles, but you slipped out of character in a few instances.	You did not display an understanding of courtroom roles, and you did not stay in character.
Team Contribution	Your positive interactions—listening to and incorporating others' opinions, seeking compromises, and following job assignments—enhanced your team's final product.	Your sporadic positive interactions—occasionally listening to and incorporating others' opinions, seeking compromises, and following job assignments—had some impact on the final product.	Your negative interactions—ignoring others' opinions, refusing to compromise, not completing your job assignment—had no positive impact on the final product.
Public Speaking	Enthusiasm, knowledge, vocal projection, pacing, and confidence marked your public speaking.	Your public speaking needs improvement in only a few of the following areas: enthusiasm, knowledge, vocal projection, pacing, and confidence.	Your public speaking needs improvement in many of the following areas: enthusiasm, knowledge, vocal projection, pacing, and confidence.
Clarity	Your language—including word choice, sentence structure, mechanics, and logic—was precise and flowed beautifully.	Your language—including word choice, sentence structure, mechanics, and logic—was precise, but was jerky in places.	Your language—including word choice, sentence structure, mechanics, and logic—was imprecise, confusing, or fuzzy.

Additional Comments:

Total Score:

LAWYERS' RUBRIC

	Excellent	Good	Needs Work
Argument	The points you made and the words you used to present them created a compelling case.	The points you made and the words you used to present them were commanding at times and weak at others.	The points you made and the words you used to present them lacked power and conviction.
Support	Your argument had rock-solid support, and your well-chosen details enhanced your argument.	Your argument showed some support, but left some holes or could be viewed as opinion.	Your argument was not supported by facts, evidence, or testimony.
Synthesis	You combined facts, testimony, and new ideas to create an original argument, and you anticipated the opposition's attack.	You combined facts, testimony, and new ideas to create a strong case, but you did not consider the opposition's attack.	You focused on only one piece of evidence or testimony and did not consider the effect that other facts could have on your case.

WITNESS RUBRIC

	Excellent	**Good**	**Needs Work**
Persuasion	The responses you made and how you worded those responses created a compelling testimony.	The responses you made and the way you worded those responses were commanding at times, but weak at others.	The responses you made and the way you worded those responses lacked power or conviction.
Support	Your testimony had rock-solid support, and your descriptions and details enhanced your story.	Your testimony showed some support, but left some holes or included what could be considered opinion.	Your testimony was not supported by facts or evidence.
Synthesis	You combined the facts of your witness statement with plausible new facts to create an original witness testimony.	You portrayed the facts of your witness statement in a credible way that did not contradict new facts.	Your confusion about your or others' witness statement facts portrayed a weak testimony.

BAILIFF RUBRIC

	Excellent	Good	Needs Work
Leadership	You took control of courtroom procedures and kept the trial running smoothly.	When prompted, you used the appropriate sentences to move the trial along.	You were confused about what your job was or how the courtroom functioned.
Organization	Your completed paperwork was organized, allowing you to remain focused and complete your tasks.	Although your paperwork was mostly complete, you had difficulty keeping track of which step was next.	Your paperwork was incomplete, and you had a great deal of difficulty keeping track of the next step.
Synthesis	As the presiding juror, you listened carefully to witnesses' testimony and directed the jury with appropriate questions on key points.	As the presiding juror, you posed some basic questions for the jury to consider but missed key points.	As the presiding juror, you did not pose appropriate questions for the jury to consider.

Lesson 5

Concepts

- Eyewitness
- Expert witness
- Proof

Materials

- Case scenarios (pp. 82–87)
- Case Analysis sheets (pp. 88–89)
- Dry-erase markers and erasers (optional)

Grade-Level Expectations

The student:
- Shows breadth of vocabulary knowledge, demonstrating understanding of word meanings or relationships by the use of words in context.
- Demonstrates initial understanding of informational texts by organizing information to show understanding.
- Uses comprehension strategies before, during, and after reading informational texts.

Student Objective

The student develops a deeper understanding of court processes by analyzing a case scenario according to the information presented.

Introduction

After reviewing any concepts you feel students may be shaky on, divide students into groups based on reading comprehension ability and distribute scenarios. Scenarios A and B are appropriate for students working at grade level, scenarios C

DOI: 10.4324/9781003236955-9

and D are appropriate for students working above grade level, and scenarios E and F are appropriate for students working at or below grade level.

Recognition

In groups, students read through their assigned scenarios aloud. Then students reread the scenarios to themselves, placing a check beside each character the first time he or she is mentioned. Students then read the scenarios to themselves for a third and final time, and students underline what they consider to be the important facts of the case.

Application

Each student completes a Case Analysis sheet.
1. Prior to distributing copies of the sheet, you may review the information it contains and discuss any confusing elements with students.
2. Students should understand the importance of backing up their points with relevant information.

Problem Solving

Students work in groups to analyze their scenarios.
1. Students share their individual analyses.
2. Each group comes to a consensus regarding the facts of the case (e.g., which evidence helps which side, which facts are murky).
3. Each group presents its case to the class.

Additional Notes

- Before allowing students to read through the scenarios, review the Case Analysis sheet to ensure that students understand which information belongs where (e.g., the difference between the facts of the case and the evidence that supports those facts).
- These case scenarios were designed to demonstrate that information can be interpreted and used differently. Rather than being cut and dry, all of the cases are debatable—student discussion about the cases should be encouraged!
- Many students enjoy reading these cases. If you see students engaging with the material, consider encouraging them to read through and discuss more than one case. We like to laminate the cases and give students dry-erase markers with which to annotate them; this way, their notes can be erased or amended, and you do not have to make so many copies of the cases.

Lesson 5

CASE SCENARIO A

Steve is a 12-year-old boy who lives in Ocean City, NJ. He received a brand-new, shiny red bicycle for his birthday on April 1. On Saturday, April 8, he got up early, planning to take a long bike ride on the boardwalk, but when he went to his garage to get his bike, it was gone. He called the police and reported the theft. After searching the garage carefully, the police detective found a torn piece of a blue sweatshirt caught on the garage door hook.

The color of the sweatshirt scrap matched the color of sweatshirts worn by students from a school on the other side of town. The police concentrated their search there. On May 1, a boy was spotted riding a red bicycle that matched the description of the one that had been stolen. Mark was picked up and questioned.

Mark explained that the bike had been a gift from his Uncle Tony, who was in the Navy. Tony had been home on leave a few weeks earlier and had given Mark the bike as a reward for getting good grades. Mark claimed that the bike was secondhand and showed the police several rust spots on the bike frame.

The police interviewed the owner of a local bike shop, who confirmed that the bike found in Mark's possession was the same model as the bike that had been stolen from Steve's garage.

The case went to court.

CASE SCENARIO B

Mary and Louise are both 14 years old, and they both live in Benson, NC. They operate an afterschool dog-walking service in their neighborhood. They started the business 2 years ago and have an excellent reputation with their clients. Last Monday afternoon, Mary arrived at the Smith residence—902 Front Street—to walk their collie, Fred. To her surprise, the front door was open. As she started to back away to go and get help, three men burst from the house holding bags of valuables, with Fred close on their heels.

Mary was unable to get a good look at their faces, but she reported that they were all wearing bright yellow sweatshirts with a parrot logo on the back. The men jumped in a waiting car and sped off. Mary called the police immediately.

The police determined that the house had been burglarized, but that whoever had done it must have had access to a key, as none of the doors had been forced open. Louise confirmed that after walking Fred that morning before school, she had locked the door when she left.

Among the items that had been stolen were several unusual necklaces. These items turned up in a pawnshop within a few weeks. The owner's description of the seller's clothing matched Mary's description of the sweatshirts worn by the men at the residence.

In Benson, NC, there is a restaurant called the Parrot Café, which sells yellow sweatshirts similar to those worn by the men in the robbery. There are three employees, Manny, Steve, and Jack, who often wear these sweatshirts. Although none of the stolen property was found in any of the men's homes, each man paid off loans at a local bank shortly after the robbery occurred.

The case went to court.

CASE SCENARIO C

Mary Smith and her husband Ron live in a quiet neighborhood in Savannah, GA. Mary is a retired teacher, and her husband works for a local insurance agency. They have lived in their present neighborhood for about 2 years and do not know their neighbors very well. Three months ago, a cat began to come to their back porch looking for food. He seemed thin, and his coat looked uncared for, with matted fur and dirt covering most of his body.

Mary grew quite fond of their visitor and decided that he needed a home. She let him into the house and began to think of him as her cat. Ron insisted that if they were going to keep this cat, they would have to take him to the veterinarian. Mary took "Sam" to the local vet, Dr. Saperstein, for a checkup. Sam needed shots and needed to be neutered. After all was said and done, the vet bill was $315. Mary also had Sam professionally groomed to get rid of his matted fur, and because Sam was a longhaired cat, this was an expensive service, with the bill totaling $45.

Sam had become a very handsome and healthy-looking cat. He wanted desperately to go back outside, so one day Mary let him out. He was gone for 2 days, and she feared the worst. On the third day, Sam returned, but he had on a new collar with a note attached that read, "If you are feeding this cat, please call 346-9285."

Mary called the number and discovered that what she had thought was a stray cat actually belonged to a neighbor, John Jensen. Mr. Jensen was anxious to have his prize Persian cat returned. Mary agreed to return the cat but insisted that Mr. Jensen split the vet and groomer bill (a total of $360) with her. Mr. Jensen was furious when he discovered that Mary had had his cat neutered, as the cat had been a source of income for Mr. Jensen through breeders' payments. He refused to give her a single penny.

Mary called her lawyer, and the case went to court.

CASE SCENARIO D

Eric Houston is a mechanic in Philadelphia, PA. He works hard and has a good reputation at the garage where he has been employed for 16 years. In April, Mr. Houston attended an outdoor festival at the Philadelphia Art Museum. Upon returning home, he discovered that his wallet was missing. He immediately called the police and reported his missing wallet. On May 25, a man from a collection agency approached Mr. Houston at work. The agency claimed that Mr. Houston had run up a debt of $25,000 on his credit card and said that they were going to repossess his Cadillac as collateral. Mr. Houston stated that he did not have a Cadillac and that they must have the wrong man. The agent, however, produced paperwork that clearly identified Mr. Houston as the debtor and said that he would take whatever car Mr. Houston was driving to help balance the debt.

Without his car, Mr. Houston would be unable to get to work. In desperation, he threatened the collection agent and made him leave the garage property. The next thing Mr. Houston knew, the police had arrived and arrested him.

In his statement, Mr. Houston said that he had not made any of the charges on the credit card, which had all been incurred between April 8 and May 4. He did admit that he had received several letters and bills about these debts, but he thought that because he had reported his wallet missing, he was not responsible for them. The creditors included the Cadillac dealership, Barmakian Jewelers, and an electronics store.

The case was taken to court.

CASE SCENARIO E

On May 17, a young woman named Mary Morgan was found at The Mall of New Hampshire with her purse filled with stolen merchandise. She claimed that she had no idea how the items had gotten there. Mary stated that she had gone to the ladies' room during her shopping trip and had left her purse unattended by the sink area. She had also tried on clothes in the women's department of a large department store and left her bag hanging in the dressing room while she exchanged items. Mary claimed that this had provided ample time for someone else to put the items in her bag.

The mall police stated that Ms. Morgan was a regular visitor to the mall. They described a past interaction with her during which she'd had an argument with a store employee regarding the store return policy. She had been arrested, but not before trying to run away from the police. When apprehended, she had been angry and insulting to the mall officers.

The case went to court.

Order in the Court © Taylor & Francis Group

CASE SCENARIO F

On July 25, the police in Atlantic City, NJ, received a 911 call at 3:00 in the morning regarding a robbery in progress at 483 Mt. Vernon Ave. Upon arriving at the scene, police observed a young man in a red shirt heading north on the street. When he saw the police car, he began to run. Police gave chase and apprehended the suspect three blocks from the scene. The suspect, Dylan Randolph, was a resident of the neighborhood. At the time of his arrest, there was no evidence on him from the robbed house.

The neighbor who had called 911, Mrs. Evan, lives across the street from the crime scene. She is an elderly lady who spends much of her day sitting in her picture window watching the comings and goings of the neighborhood residents. When she saw a man dressed all in black break a side window in her neighbor's, house she called the police.

The police found a duffel bag about a block south of the house filled with items identified by the house's owner, Mrs. Jones, as stolen items. Also in the bag were a black hooded sweatshirt and a pair of black gloves.

The case went to court.

CASE ANALYSIS

Step 1: Identify the main characters.

Plaintiff: _____

Defendant: _____

Step 2: Identify the facts of the case. Who did what to whom? List the sequence of events in chronological order (what came first, what came second, and so on):

_____

_____

_____

_____

_____

_____

_____

Step 3: Identify the supporting evidence. How do you know that the events you listed in Step 2 actually happened? List the evidence you have:

_____

_____

_____

_____

_____

_____

_____

Name:_____ Date: _____

Step 4: Identify potential witnesses. List the people who could testify regarding specific facts, and state whether each person's testimony would help the plaintiff's case or the defendant's case.

Name	Testimony	Plaintiff or Defendant

Lesson 6

Concepts

- Case analysis
- Court strategy
- Word choice

Materials

- Statement of the Facts sheet (pp. 93–95)
- Witness Statement sheets (pp. 96–103)
- Role Assignments and Materials Needed sheet (p. 104)
- Role-specific handouts (pp. 105–126)
- Materials from Lessons 3 and 4 (Instructions for Witnesses sheet, p. 52; rubrics, pp. 76–79)

Student Objective

The student demonstrates an understanding of court processes by adopting a role in a trial based on real-world events.

Introduction

After reading aloud the Statement of Facts sheet for the class, assign roles for the trial.

Recognition

Students meet in small groups according to their assigned roles and read through the appropriate role-specific handouts.

DOI: 10.4324/9781003236955-10

Application

Students prepare for their roles.
1. They complete their role-specific handouts.
2. They plan their strategies and conference with each other, seeking teacher assistance if necessary.

Problem Solving

The students trade off in teams to conduct the trial.
1. Each team conducts the trial, with team members playing their assigned roles.
2. The alternate team acts as the jury when it is not conducting the trial.

Grade-Level Expectations

The student:
- Shows breadth of vocabulary knowledge, demonstrating understanding of word meanings or relationships by the use of words in context.
- Demonstrates initial understanding of informational texts by organizing information to show understanding.
- Uses comprehension strategies before, during, and after reading informational texts.

Additional Notes

- This second trial is conducted in essentially the same manner as the first. Instead of basing their testimony on fairy tales, the witnesses will receive prompt sheets; these will be considered part of the facts of the case, and witnesses will use them to write their letters to the judge.
- Whereas the first trial focused on a simpler case with which students were already familiar, and for which stakes were low, much of this case's information will be new to students and is more relevant to their daily lives. For this trial, the plaintiff is being tried for music piracy. As opposed to the fairy tale theme of the previous trial, the theme of this trial—whether or not downloading music is a crime—is current and relevant to students. The copyright law used in the Statement of Facts sheet is taken from actual law. We have found that this trial's incorporation of real laws presents many teachable moments with regard to music piracy. Students seem to believe that all music is free, and we often have to explain the concepts of royalties and copyrights.
- Although the demands of the various roles are similar to what they were in the first trial, it is a good idea to give students the chance to play new roles. Because there are more witness roles in this trial than in the previous ones, and because it is hoped that students will all be comfortable by now with the courtroom procedures, we usually do not assign a bailiff in this second trial,

allowing all students to play more involved roles (i.e., witnesses and lawyers). Rather, a member of the jury steps up to serve as the bailiff. Of course, you can still elect to assign a student to the bailiff role, particularly if you have one student who is very reluctant or who lacks confidence. The plaintiff, the defendant, and the witnesses are only in charge of knowing their own stories, making these roles suitable for students in the middle. The lawyer roles are the most complicated. Students playing these roles must truly synthesize the information. Clearly, this trial format works well with a heterogeneous group. However, it is certainly also suitable for a homogenous group, particularly a group of high-ability students, who can infuse the roles with more creativity and detail.

- With the first trial, but especially with this one, there is a lot of necessary paperwork. We find it useful to provide a file box containing extra copies of handouts in case students need them.

- Each lawyer team must have a complete set of the witness statements. Although lawyers can speak directly with their own witnesses, the only information that they can gain from the opposing witnesses—whom they will cross-examine—comes from these witness statements. They should be allowed to have the witness statements on hand as they are cross-examining the opposing witnesses so that they can check for accuracy in the witnesses' testimony. The witnesses, however, should not be allowed to have their statements in front of them while they are on the stand, as they should have to memorize the facts of the case.

- If students are having difficulty, we sometimes encourage them to confer with the students playing their same roles for the other team (e.g., defense lawyers can speak with defense lawyers).

STATEMENT OF THE FACTS

FEDERAL DISTRICT COURT

Million Hits Recording Company,
Plaintiffs,
v.
Lee Sydney,
Defendant

The following facts are agreed to by all parties in this case:

Lee Sydney was a resident of Outer Creek, MI, a town of approximately 5,000, from birth until 1 year ago. At that time, Lee's family moved to Turnsborough, a suburb of Detroit. Lee is 17 years old, is currently a senior at Turnsborough High School, and is the youngest of three children, with an older brother and sister who are currently both away at college. Lee lives with one parent, Robin Sydney, an accountant who works in the city.

Lee is an honor-roll student who is involved in the high school band. During Lee's first year at Turnsborough High, navigating the school's social groups was difficult, but over the summer, making friends was easier. For the last 6 months, Lee has been very involved with a particular group of popular students. Robin Sydney, along with Lee's teachers, felt that adjustment to the new school and town was finally taking place.

When Lee and Robin first moved to Turnsborough, Lee was allowed to purchase a new computer and subsequently developed strong computer skills, becoming highly efficient in computer knowledge and use. Lee also owns a cell phone and a 60-gigabyte mp3 player. When the police investigated this case, they lawfully obtained a warrant for these electronic devices and had their contents examined by the Detroit Crime Lab at the request of the Turnsborough Police Department. Lee's computer was found to have 567 songs saved in its memory, and the mp3 player contained these same 567 songs, as well as an additional 146 titles. In addition, the computer contained downloaded copies of 54 movies. Lee's cell phone text messages were transcribed and have been entered as evidence. They show clearly that Lee was sharing the previously described collection of music and movies with friends.

Lee has been charged with violating copyright laws by illegally downloading and distributing copyrighted material without securing permission from the copyright owner. Specifically, the charge is violation of the following sections of copyright law:

§ 506. Criminal offenses

(a) CRIMINAL INFRINGEMENT. —

(1) IN GENERAL. — Any person who willfully infringes a copyright shall be punished as provided under section 2319 of title 18, if the infringement was committed —

(A) for purposes of commercial advantage or private financial gain;

(B) by the reproduction or distribution, including by electronic means, during any 180-day period, of 1 or more copies or phonorecords of 1 or more copyrighted works, which have a total retail value of more than $1,000; or

(C) by the distribution of a work being prepared for commercial distribution, by making it available on a computer network accessible to members of the public, if such person knew or should have known that the work was intended for commercial distribution.

(2) EVIDENCE. — For purposes of this subsection, evidence of reproduction or distribution of a copyrighted work, by itself, shall not be sufficient to establish willful infringement of a copyright.

§ 2319. Criminal infringement of a copyright

(a) Whoever violates section 506(a) (relating to criminal offenses) of title 17 shall be punished as provided in subsections (b) and (c) of this section and such penalties shall be in addition to any other provisions of title 17 or any other law.

(b) Any person who commits an offense under section 506(a)(1) of title 17 —

(1) shall be imprisoned not more than 5 years, or fined in the amount set forth in this title, or both, if the offense consists of the reproduction or distribution, including by electronic means, during any 180-day period, of at least 10 copies or phonorecords, of 1 or more copyrighted works, which have a total retail value of more than $2,500;

(2) shall be imprisoned not more than 10 years, or fined in the amount set forth in this title, or both, if the offense is a second or subsequent offense under paragraph (1); and

(3) shall be imprisoned not more than 1 year, or fined in the amount set forth in this title, or both, in any other case.

(c) Any person who commits an offense under section 506(a)(2) of title 17, United States Code —

(1) shall be imprisoned not more than 3 years, or fined in the amount set forth in this title, or both, if the offense consists of the reproduction or distribution of 10 or more copies or phonorecords of 1 or more copyrighted works, which have a total retail value of $2,500 or more;

(2) shall be imprisoned not more than 6 years, or fined in the amount set forth in this title, or both, if the offense is a second or subsequent offense under paragraph (1); and

Given the total number of infringements, the prosecution is asking for the maximum penalty in this case.

Lee and the lawyers for the defense intend to argue that while Lee may have illegally downloaded items from the Internet, this was done without the knowledge that it was illegal, and Lee never distributed or profited in any way from this activity. They will also argue that because the songs on the mp3 player are the same songs as the ones on the computer, the songs should not be counted twice.

The burden of proof lies with the prosecution.

In the Case of
Million Hits Recording Company
v.
Lee Sydney

WITNESSES FOR THE PLAINTIFF
Alex Smith, C.E.O., Million Hits Recording Co., plaintiff
Devyn Miller, industry expert*
J. J. Lopez, songwriter
Chris Swansey, crime lab representative

WITNESSES FOR THE DEFENDANT
Lee Sydney, defendant
Robin Sydney, parent/guardian of defendant
Sandy Lake, friend of defendant
Riley Bain, industry expert*

*It is agreed that these witnesses may serve as experts in the field of determining the value of recorded materials.

WITNESS STATEMENT

ALEX SMITH
C.E.O., Million Hits Recording Company, Plaintiff

My name is Alex Smith, and I am 42 years old. I am the C.E.O. of Million Hits Recording Company.

Since 1999, the sales of recorded music have shown a clear downward trend. At the same time, sales of blank CD-R disks have been skyrocketing. What happened in 1999? File sharing became widely popular.

The actual cost of sound recording piracy hurts not only U.S. producers and distributors of sound recordings—owners of intellectual property—but also American consumers and taxpayers. Specifically, as Siwek (2007) showed, piracy has the following disastrous effects:

1. Due to global and domestic piracy of sound recordings, the U.S. economy loses $12.5 billion in annual total output, including revenue and other measures of economic performance.

2. Due to sound recording piracy, the American economy loses 71,060 jobs. Of these jobs, 26,860 are lost from the sound recording industry or from retail industries, while 44,200 are lost from related U.S. industries.

3. Due to sound recording piracy, American workers lose $2.7 billion in annual earnings. Of this number, $1.1 billion are lost from workers in the sound recording industry and in related retail industries, while $1.6 billion are lost from workers in other American industries.

4. Due to sound recording piracy, American federal, state, and local governments lose, at minimum, $422 million in annual tax revenues. Of this amount, $291 million is lost in personal income taxes, while $131 million in corporate income and production taxes is lost.

No company likes taking its own customers to court. But when your product is being stolen on a regular basis, there comes a time when you have to take appropriate action. We simply cannot allow online piracy to continue destroying the livelihoods of artists, musicians, songwriters, retailers, and others in the music industry.

Illegal downloading of music is theft, pure and simple. Illegal downloading robs songwriters, artists, and the industry that supports them of their property and their livelihoods. Ironically, those who steal music are stealing from the creative minds of the present and future. We must end this destructive cycle now.

_____

Alex Smith, C.E.O., Million Hits Recording Company

Reference

Siwek, S. (2007.) *The true cost of sound recording piracy to the U.S. economy.* Institute for Policy Innovation. Retrieved from http://www.ipi.org/IPI/IPIPublications.nsf/Public ationLookupFullText/5C2EE3D2107A4C228625733E0053A1F4

WITNESS STATEMENT

DEVYN MILLER
Marketing Analyst, Million Hits Recording Company, Expert Witness

My name is Devyn Miller, and I am 48 years old. I am a marketing analyst employed by Million Hits Record Company. I have worked with the company for 12 years. I received my bachelor's and master's degrees in marketing from University of California, Los Angeles. Part of my job is to investigate, and place a monetary figure on, how much revenue Million Hits Recording Company loses every year due to the pirating of its materials. In-house counsel at the company contacted me and asked if I could put a dollar amount on the number of their songs that the defendant downloaded. I said that I could.

Lee Sydney was found to be in possession of some 1,280 songs saved on electronic equipment. Lee Sydney allegedly downloaded some 713 songs total (found on two separate devices) and some 54 movies. Using an estimate of $1 per song and $10 per movie, the total comes to $1,280 for the songs and $540 for the movies, or some $1,820 total. This is not counting, however, lost CD revenues that occurred because the defendant did not have to purchase an entire CD once a particular song was downloaded, but I was not asked to investigate that aspect of the claim.

———————————————————

Devyn Miller, Marketing Analyst,
Million Hits Recording Company

WITNESS STATEMENT

J. J. LOPEZ
Songwriter Under Contract With Million Hits Recording Company

My name is J. J. Lopez, and I am 29 years old. Many people feel that when they steal a song on the Internet, it is a victimless crime. But I am here to tell you that I am a victim of this crime. I wrote many of the songs that the defendant downloaded illegally and shared happily with friends. This may have been fun for them, but it essentially took money out of my pocket. Every time one of my songs is sold, I receive royalty income from the sale. Songwriters don't get salaries—they pay their rent, their medical bills, and their children's educational expenses with royalty income. That income has been seriously impacted by illegal downloading. The fact is, many artists' incomes have been reduced so drastically that they have reassessed their careers as songwriters.

If you engage in illegal downloading—that is, if you download a song without paying for it—you are a common thief. If you allow your children to engage in illegal downloading, you are telling them that thievery is acceptable. If you are a college administrator and you turn a blind eye to illegal downloading on your campus, you are encouraging larceny in the hallowed halls of education.

_____

J. J. Lopez, Songwriter

WITNESS STATEMENT

CHRIS SWANSEY
Technology Forensics Expert, Detroit Crime Lab

My name is Chris Swansey, and I am 36 years old. I have been employed by the Detroit Crime Lab as an expert in technological forensics for the past 5 years.

On May 10, the crime lab received a request from the Turnsborough Police Department to investigate the materials on electronic devices found in possession of the defendant, Lee Sydney.

I personally examined the evidence and found a total of 567 songs on the hard drive of Sydney's computer. The same 567 songs were found on the mp3 player belonging to Syndey, along with an additional 146 songs. The computer belonging to the defendant contained 54 movies.

In tracing the origins of the songs and movies through the associated IP addresses, I was able to ascertain beyond doubt that these materials had been illegally downloaded.

———————————————————

Detective Chris Swansey,
Crime Lab Expert

WITNESS STATEMENT

LEE SYDNEY
Plaintiff

My name is Lee Sydney, and I am 17 years old. I am currently a senior at Turnsborough High School. I live with Robin Sydney. I have two older siblings who are away at college. I moved to Turnsborough about a year ago. The summer after we moved here was really hard for me. I didn't know anyone in the area, and living in a big city overwhelmed me. I managed to get through the summer, because my sister and brother were home from college. It felt like my life was over when September came and they left and high school started.

Most of the kids in my school had known each other all their lives. It was very difficult to be the new kid. The fall semester of last year was miserable for me. I tried to make friends by joining the band, but I wasn't very successful. I was never happier to see my siblings than when they came home for Thanksgiving.

Over the holiday, I found my brother listening to some new music. He showed me the site online where he had found it. The site that he showed me was a pay-as-you-go one, but I soon found sites where you did not have to pay. It was a whole new world opening up for me. I had no idea that this was illegal. Because the music was posted on the Internet, I thought it was copyright free.

When I went back to school, I started asking around to see if everyone was using the Internet for music. A few days later, the most popular person in school came up to me and asked me how to find the music on the Internet. I promised to do a demonstration after school at my house. We became friends, and finally the social world of Turnsborough High began to open up for me. Before long, a whole group of my new friends would come to my house after school. It was the perfect place to hang out, because I was alone until 6:00 every night. We weren't doing anything bad, like drugs—we were just listening to music and burning CDs. Then we found some sites where we could download movies, so we started to use those sites as well. None of us knew that what we were doing was illegal. None of those sites made any statements about the materials being copyrighted. The sites only prohibited users from selling the material to other people. We thought that as long as we weren't making a profit on the CDs, we were within the law.

On May 9, the police showed up at my school and arrested me. I was shocked and humiliated. Suddenly, all my new friends besides Sandy disappeared. I guess when the going gets tough, you find out who your friends really are.

_____

Lee Sydney, Defendant

WITNESS STATEMENT

ROBIN SYDNEY

Parent/Guardian of the Plaintiff

My name is Robin Sydney. I am 45 years old. I live at 426 Pleasant Dr., Turnsborough, MI. I am employed as an accountant by the firm of Bailey, Bates, and Jones in Detroit. I have been employed there for 1 year.

I moved my three children and myself to Turnsborough after my divorce became final. I was lucky to find a good job in Detroit and began commuting into the city every day. Although this was not an ideal situation, being that Lee is in high school, I thought that living in the suburbs would be easier than living in the city proper.

Lee has always been a responsible person and a good student. I was not concerned about the possibility of Lee getting into trouble. The first several months we lived here were hard—it's difficult to make friends in a new place. I was thrilled to hear that after Thanksgiving, new friends had begun visiting the house after school. I trusted my child and believed that this group of kids did not smoke, drink, or do drugs—and indeed, that was true.

Lee has always been very adept in terms of computer skills—far more skilled than I—so it made sense that a lot of Lee's afterschool activities involved the Internet. I did not realize that downloading music was illegal any more than Lee did. I bought the mp3 player in question as a Christmas gift—what parent doesn't want to encourage a love of music?

Lee is a responsible young person who is being used by the music industry to make a point. If these songs are available for free download on the Internet, shouldn't the law be going after the sites that offer free music, rather than the minors who are using those sites in good faith?

_____

Robin Sydney,
Parent/Guardian of the Defendant

WITNESS STATEMENT

SANDY LAKE
Student at Turnsborough High School

My name is Sandy Lake, and I am 18 years old. I am a senior at Turnsborough High School. Lee Sydney is a friend of mine, and I was one of the students who frequently hung out at the Sydney residence after school.

I didn't meet Lee until after Thanksgiving. One of my soccer teammates asked me if I wanted to go hang out with a bunch of our friends after school one day in early December. I went to Lee's house for the first time that day. It was innocent stuff—Lee had found some sites that allowed you to download music for free. Everyone thought it was pretty cool, and we enjoyed listening to new and different music. It wasn't long before different people started asking Lee to burn them CDs of their favorite bands. We knew we couldn't sell the CDs, but we didn't know that sharing them was illegal.

Everyone was shocked the day the police showed up at school. We felt really bad for Lee. Most of the kids pretended not to know Lee. But I don't think it's right to prosecute someone for stealing if that person never made a profit. We weren't trying to hurt anyone, and there were no warnings on the websites to inform us that what we were doing was illegal.

Since Lee got in trouble, I have read the law, and it says that you have to make a profit or download over a certain number of songs for it to qualify as a crime. Lee did not download over the limit. The prosecution is counting the copies that Lee had on an mp3 player as separate songs, which isn't fair—they were the same songs, just on a different device.

_____

Sandy Lake, Student

WITNESS STATEMENT

RILEY BAIN
Marketing Analyst, *Rocking Tunes* Magazine, Expert Witness

My name is Riley Bain, and I am 49 years old. I am employed as a marketing analyst by *Rocking Tunes* Magazine. I have been employed there for 8 years.

Our magazine does not advocate illegally downloading music or movies from peer-to-peer (P2P) network sites. However, we disagree with the music industry in terms of the value of pirated materials. Part of my job is to analyze the market value of songs in order to make bids to recording companies; my company often pays so that we can offer songs as legal downloads on our website for free—this serves to generate excitement among our readers for different artists, songs, and albums, just as radio stations once were used to popularize a new record.

In May of this year, lawyers for the defendant, Lee Sydney, contacted me and asked me to review Devyn Miller's calculations for the dollar amount of the alleged loss associated with the defendant's downloading of music and movies.

I agreed to do so and drew the following conclusions: In a technical sense, Miller's findings are accurate, but in a practical sense, they are not. This discrepancy stems from the way the loss numbers were calculated. Miller based these numbers on the average price of all movies and songs. In other words, several statisticians averaged the prices of thousands of movies and thousands of songs. The result of this averaging was the conclusion that each song is worth about $1, and each movie is worth about $10.

When one considers the actual retail value of the songs and movies that the defendant downloaded, their costs average much less—roughly $0.30 per song and $7 per movie. The defendant downloaded some 713 songs total and some 54 movies, which would have resulted in losses totaling $213.90 for the songs and $378 for the movies, or $591.90 in combination.

While it is true that Miller employed the more commonly accepted method of calculating losses, the method I used to arrive at my conclusions is sanctioned by several leading journals and is slowly being employed in more and more situations. This is because it is simply more accurate, as it employs the actual retail value of the products in question, rather than general averages.

Riley Bain, Market Analyst,
Rocking Tunes Magazine

ROLE ASSIGNMENTS AND
MATERIALS NEEDED

STUDENT NAME	ROLE	MATERIALS	STATEMENT(S)
PROSECUTION			
	Alex Smith PLAINTIFF	Witness Prompt	Witness Statement
	PROSECUTOR #1	Prosecution Packet	All Witness Statements
	PROSECUTOR #2	Prosecution Packet	All Witness Statements
	Devyn Miller WITNESS	Witness Prompt	Witness Statement
	J. J. Lopez WITNESS	Witness Prompt	Witness Statement
	Chris Swansey WITNESS	Witness Prompt	Witness Statement
DEFENSE			
	Lee Sydney DEFENDANT	Witness Prompt	Witness Statement
	DEFENSE ATTORNEY #1	Defense Packet	All Witness Statements
	DEFENSE ATTORNEY #2	Defense Packet	All Witness Statements
	Robin Sydney WITNESS	Witness Prompt	Witness Statement
	Sandy Lake WITNESS	Witness Prompt	Witness Statement
	Riley Bain WITNESS	Witness Prompt	Witness Statement

Instructions for Prosecuting Attorneys

As a member of the prosecution team, you have the job of proving beyond a shadow of a doubt that Lee Sydney is guilty of the charges filed. It is crucial that you establish a timeline of events and provide evidence to prove your points.

The prosecution team is responsible for preparing the following components of the trial:

- the **opening statement**;
- the **direct examination** of witnesses (you have four witnesses to rely on— Alex Smith, Devyn Miller, J. J. Lopez, and Chris Swansey);
- the **cross-examination** of witnesses (you have the opportunity to cross- examine the defense's four witnesses—Lee Sydney, Robin Sydney, Sandy Lake, and Riley Bain); and
- the **closing statement**.

Meet as a team and divide up the labor to make the most of your time. For the safety of the community, it is very important that you are successful in sending a strong message that illegal downloading is stealing!

Name:_____ Date: _____

OPENING STATEMENT: PROSECUTION

Case Title: *Million Hits Recording Company v. Lee Sydney*
Attorney Presenting:

IMPORTANT POINTS

_____

_____

_____

_____

_____

_____

_____

_____

_____

_____

_____

_____

_____

_____

_____

_____

Order in the Court © Taylor & Francis Group

DIRECT EXAMINATION OF
WITNESS #1: PROSECUTION

Case Title: *Million Hits Recording Company v. Lee Sydney*
Attorney Presenting:
Witness: Alex Smith

Questions:	Important Points
1. _____ _____ _____	
2. _____ _____ _____	
3. _____ _____ _____	
4. _____ _____ _____	
5. _____ _____ _____	

DIRECT EXAMINATION OF
WITNESS #2: PROSECUTION

Case Title: *Million Hits Recording Company v. Lee Sydney*
Attorney Presenting:
Witness: Devyn Miller

Questions:	Important Points
1. _____ _____ _____ 2. _____ _____ _____ 3. _____ _____ _____ 4. _____ _____ _____ 5. _____ _____ _____	

DIRECT EXAMINATION OF
WITNESS #3: PROSECUTION

Case Title: *Million Hits Recording Company v. Lee Sydney*
Attorney Presenting:
Witness: J. J. Lopez

Questions:	Important Points
1. _____ _____ _____	
2. _____ _____ _____	
3. _____ _____ _____	
4. _____ _____ _____	
5. _____ _____ _____	

Name:_____ Date: _____

DIRECT EXAMINATION OF
WITNESS #4: PROSECUTION

Case Title: *Million Hits Recording Company v. Lee Sydney*
Attorney Presenting:
Witness: Chris Swansey

Questions:	Important Points
1. _____ _____ _____	
2. _____ _____ _____	
3. _____ _____ _____	
4. _____ _____ _____	
5. _____ _____ _____	

Order in the Court © Taylor & Francis Group

CROSS-EXAMINATION OF
WITNESS #5: PROSECUTION

Case Title: *Million Hits Recording Company v. Lee Sydney*
Attorney Presenting:
Witness: Lee Sydney

Questions*:	Important Points
1. _____ _____ _____	
2. _____ _____ _____	
3. _____ _____ _____	
4. _____ _____ _____	
5. _____ _____ _____	

*Additional questions based on direct examination testimony and the witness's responses to the above questions may be added during the trial.

Name:_____ Date: _____

CROSS-EXAMINATION OF
WITNESS #6: PROSECUTION

Case Title: *Million Hits Recording Company v. Lee Sydney*
Attorney Presenting:
Witness: Robin Sydney

Questions*:	Important Points
1. _____	
_____	
_____	
2. _____	
_____	
_____	
3. _____	
_____	
_____	
4. _____	
_____	
_____	
5. _____	
_____	
_____	

*Additional questions based on direct examination testimony and the witness's responses to the above questions may be added during the trial.

Order in the Court © Taylor & Francis Group

CROSS-EXAMINATION OF
WITNESS #7: PROSECUTION

Case Title: *Million Hits Recording Company v. Lee Sydney*
Attorney Presenting:
Witness: Sandy Lake

Questions*:	Important Points
1. _____ _____ _____	
2. _____ _____ _____	
3. _____ _____ _____	
4. _____ _____ _____	
5. _____ _____ _____	

*Additional questions based on direct examination testimony and the witness's responses to the above questions may be added during the trial.

Name:_____ Date: _____

CROSS-EXAMINATION OF
WITNESS #8: PROSECUTION

Case Title: *Million Hits Recording Company v. Lee Sydney*
Attorney Presenting:
Witness: Riley Bain

Questions*:	Important Points
1. _____ _____ _____	
2. _____ _____ _____	
3. _____ _____ _____	
4. _____ _____ _____	
5. _____ _____ _____	

*Additional questions based on direct examination testimony and the witness's responses to the above questions may be added during the trial.

Name:_____ Date: _____

CLOSING STATEMENT: PROSECUTION

Case Title: *Million Hits Recording Company v. Lee Sydney*
Attorney Presenting:

IMPORTANT POINTS

_____

_____

_____

_____

_____

_____

_____

_____

_____

_____

_____

_____

_____

_____

_____

_____

Instructions for Defense Attorneys

As a member of the defense team, it is your job to show reasonable doubt that Lee Sydney is guilty of the charges filed. It is crucial for you to show that the music industry is being unfairly vindictive towards a minor.

The defense team is responsible for preparing the following components of the trial.

- the **opening statement**;
- the **direct examination** of witnesses (you have four witnesses to rely on—Lee Sydney, Robin Sydney, Sandy Lake, and Riley Bain);
- the **cross-examination** of witnesses (you have the opportunity to cross-examine the prosecution's four witnesses—Alex Smith, Devyn Miller, J. J. Lopez, and Chris Swansey); and
- the **closing statement**.

Meet as a team and divide up the labor to make the most of your time. In the interests of justice, it is essential that you prove the innocence of this young person.

Name:_____ Date: _____

OPENING STATEMENT: DEFENSE

Case Title: *Million Hits Recording Company v. Lee Sydney*
Attorney Presenting:

IMPORTANT POINTS

_____

_____

_____

_____

_____

_____

_____

_____

_____

_____

_____

_____

_____

_____

_____

_____

Name:_____ Date: _____

CROSS-EXAMINATION OF
WITNESS #1: DEFENSE

Case Title: *Million Hits Recording Company v. Lee Sydney*
Attorney Presenting:
Witness: Alex Smith

Questions*:	Important Points
1. _____ _____ _____	
2. _____ _____ _____	
3. _____ _____ _____	
4. _____ _____ _____	
5. _____ _____ _____	

*Additional questions based on direct examination testimony and the witness's responses to the above questions may be added during the trial.

Order in the Court © Taylor & Francis Group

Name:_____ Date: _____

CROSS-EXAMINATION OF
WITNESS #2: DEFENSE

Case Title: *Million Hits Recording Company v. Lee Sydney*
Attorney Presenting:
Witness: Devyn Miller

Questions*:	Important Points
1. _____ _____ _____	
2. _____ _____ _____	
3. _____ _____ _____	
4. _____ _____ _____	
5. _____ _____ _____	

*Additional questions based on direct examination testimony and the witness's responses to the above questions may be added during the trial.

Name:_____ Date: _____

CROSS-EXAMINATION OF
WITNESS #3: DEFENSE

....

Case Title: *Million Hits Recording Company v. Lee Sydney*
Attorney Presenting:
Witness: J. J. Lopez

Questions*:	Important Points
1. _____ _____ _____	
2. _____ _____ _____	
3. _____ _____ _____	
4. _____ _____ _____	
5. _____ _____ _____	

*Additional questions based on direct examination testimony and the witness's responses to the above questions may be added during the trial.

Order in the Court © Taylor & Francis Group

CROSS-EXAMINATION OF
WITNESS #4: DEFENSE

Case Title: *Million Hits Recording Company v. Lee Sydney*
Attorney Presenting:
Witness: Chris Swansey

Questions*:	Important Points
1. _____ _____ _____	
2. _____ _____ _____	
3. _____ _____ _____	
4. _____ _____ _____	
5. _____ _____ _____	

*Additional questions based on direct examination testimony and the witness's responses to the above questions may be added during the trial.

DIRECT EXAMINATION OF
WITNESS #5: DEFENSE

Case Title: *Million Hits Recording Company v. Lee Sydney*
Attorney Presenting:
Witness: Lee Sydney

Questions:	Important Points
1. _____ _____ _____	
2. _____ _____ _____	
3. _____ _____ _____	
4. _____ _____ _____	
5. _____ _____ _____	

Order in the Court © Taylor & Francis Group

DIRECT EXAMINATION OF
WITNESS #6: DEFENSE

Case Title: *Million Hits Recording Company v. Lee Sydney*
Attorney Presenting:
Witness: Robin Sydney

Questions:	Important Points
1. _____ _____ _____	
2. _____ _____ _____	
3. _____ _____ _____	
4. _____ _____ _____	
5. _____ _____ _____	

Name:_____ Date: _____

DIRECT EXAMINATION OF
WITNESS #7: DEFENSE

Case Title: *Million Hits Recording Company v. Lee Sydney*
Attorney Presenting:
Witness: Sandy Lake

Questions:	Important Points
1. _____ _____ _____	
2. _____ _____ _____	
3. _____ _____ _____	
4. _____ _____ _____	
5. _____ _____ _____	

Order in the Court © Taylor & Francis Group

DIRECT EXAMINATION OF
WITNESS #8: PROSECUTION

Case Title: *Million Hits Recording Company v. Lee Sydney*
Attorney Presenting:
Witness: Riley Bain

Questions:	Important Points
1. _____ _____ _____	
2. _____ _____ _____	
3. _____ _____ _____	
4. _____ _____ _____	
5. _____ _____ _____	

Name:_____ Date: _____

CLOSING STATEMENT: DEFENSE

Case Title: *Million Hits Recording Company v. Lee Sydney*
Attorney Presenting:

IMPORTANT POINTS

_____

_____

_____

_____

_____

_____

_____

_____

_____

_____

_____

_____

_____

_____

_____

_____

_____

Order in the Court © Taylor & Francis Group

Lesson 7

Concepts

- Self-assessment
- Reflecting on learning experiences
- Constructive criticism

Materials

- Measures of Academic Outcomes sheet (p. 129)

Student Objective

The student reflects on the mock trial experience and evaluates his or her performance.

Introduction

Lead a discussion debriefing the class on the two trials. How were they alike? How were they different? What did students learn from one to the next? What were students' strengths, and what did they find more challenging? What were their favorite parts?

Recognition

Students should discuss the trials among themselves, with students who served on the jury during a given trial providing constructive criticism to those students who played courtroom roles in that trial. Students should also be given the opportunity to review their graded rubrics from the two trials.

Application

Students demonstrate what they have learned throughout the unit.
1. You may wish to conference with students after giving them back their rubrics.

DOI: 10.4324/9781003236955-11

2. Students complete the definitions portion of the Measures of Academic Outcomes sheet.

Problem Solving

Students reflect on their experiences in the unit.
1. Students complete the self-assessment portion of the Measures of Academic Outcomes sheet.
2. You could choose the conferencing option in place of this section, debriefing with students individually in an interview format to discuss their performance and experiences.

Grade-Level Expectations

The student:
- Shows breadth of vocabulary knowledge, demonstrating understanding of word meanings or relationships by the use of words in context.
- Demonstrates initial understanding of informational texts by organizing information to show understanding.
- Uses comprehension strategies before, during, and after reading informational texts.

Additional Notes

- If your students are unaccustomed to using rubrics, they may simply look at their grades without looking at your feedback. Be sure to review rubrics with students before and after handing them back. Often, individual conferencing works well in order to show students where they showed strength and where they need improvement. It is also important to emphasize how the skills they used in the courtroom, such as thinking on their feet, persuading, and offering evidence, will be important throughout their academic and real-life careers. This topic can be incorporated into conversation.
- You can use what students have learned from the courtroom format to reinforce the concepts of other subjects, such as persuasive writing. Remind students of the importance of evidence, offering summary in openings and closings, and making persuasive statements.
- Similarly, once students have mastered the concepts of the unit, you can use the trial format for any material that can be debated (e.g., for current events, for novel studies). This format is often ideal for engaging students.
- We have used this unit very successfully in conjunction with *What's Your Opinion?* (a debate unit). We like to use *Order in the Court* in the fall to set the stage for *What's Your Opinion?* in the spring.
- This is one of our students' favorite units. They often ask to repeat the unit later in the year! It is always fascinating to watch the students realize how much they have learned without realizing it. We once had a student declare that the experience had been "kind of like trick learning"!

Lesson 7

MEASURES OF ACADEMIC OUTCOMES

Definitions

Take out a separate sheet of paper and write your name on it. Using as many words as possible from the word bank, describe the sequence of a trial and the roles and responsibilities of the people involved.

Opening Statement	Judge
Direct Examination	Jury
Cross-Examination	Bailiff
Closing Statement	Prosecuting Attorney
Plaintiff	Defense Attorney
Defendant	Witness

Self-Assessment and Reflection

Answer the following questions, using the back of this sheet or extra paper if necessary.

1. In the trial of *Ms. Petunia Pig v. Mr. B. B. Wolf*, my role was:

   _____

2. After reviewing my graded rubric for this trial, I think I did very well with:

   _____

   _____

3. If I could perform in this trial again, I would improve by:

   _____

   _____

4. In the trial of *Million Hits Recording Company v. Lee Sydney*, my role was:

   _____

   _____

5. After reviewing my graded rubric for this trial, I think I did very well with:

    _____

    _____

6. If I could perform in this trial again, I would improve by:

    _____

    _____

7. Please share your comments (likes, dislikes, suggestions, and so on) about this unit. Be specific!

    _____

    _____

Order in the Court © Taylor & Francis Group

Appendix
Student Context Rubric

The Student Context Rubric (SCR) is intended for use by the classroom teacher as a tool to help in the identification of students of masked potential. This term, *masked potential*, refers to students who are gifted, but are frequently not identified because their behaviors are not displayed to best advantage by traditional methods. The SCR was designed to be used with this series of units and the authentic performance assessments that accompany them. Although you may choose to run the units without using the SCR, you may find the rubric helpful for keeping records of student behaviors.

The units serve as platforms for the display of student behaviors, while the SCR is an instrument that teachers can use to record those behaviors when making observations. The rubric requires the observer to record the frequency of gifted behaviors, but there is also the option to note that the student demonstrates the behavior with particular intensity. In this way, the rubric is subjective and requires careful observation and consideration.

It is recommended that an SCR be completed for each student prior to the application of a unit, and once again upon completion of the unit. In this way, teachers will be reminded of behaviors to look for during the unit—particularly those behaviors that we call *loophole behaviors*, which may indicate giftedness but are often misinterpreted or overlooked. (For instance, a student's verbal ability can be missed if he or she uses it to spin wild lies about having neglected to complete an assignment.) Therefore, the SCR allows teachers to be aware of—and to document—high-ability behavior even if it is masked or used in nontraditional ways. The mechanism also provides a method for tracking changes in teachers' perceptions of their students, not only while students are working on the Interactive Discovery-Based Units for High-Ability Learners, but also while they are engaged in traditional classroom activities.

In observing student behaviors, you might consider some of the following questions after completing a lesson:

- Was there anyone or anything that surprised you today?
- Did a particular student jump out at you today?
- Did someone come up with a unique or unusual idea today?
- Was there a moment in class today when you saw a lightbulb go on? Did it involve an individual, a small group, or the class as a whole?
- In reviewing written responses after a class discussion, were you surprised by anyone (either because he or she was quiet during the discussion but had good written ideas, or because he or she was passionate in the discussion but did not write with the same passion)?
- Did any interpersonal issues affect the classroom today? If so, how were these issues resolved?
- Did the lesson go as planned today? Were there any detours?
- Is there a student whom you find yourself thinking or worrying about outside of school?
- Are there students in your classroom who seem to be on a rollercoaster of learning—"on" one day, but "off" the next?
- Are your students different outside of the classroom? In what ways are they different?
- Are there students who refuse to engage with the project?
- During a class performance, did the leadership of a group change when students got in front of their peers?
- Did your students generate new ideas today?
- What was the energy like in your class today? Did you provide the energy, or did the students?
- How long did it take the students to engage today?

Ideally, multiple observers complete the SCR for each student. If a gifted and talented specialist is available, we recommend that he or she assist. By checking off the appropriate marks to describe student behaviors, and by completing the scoring chart, participants generate quantifiable data that can be used in advocating for students who would benefit from scaffolded services. **In terms of students' scores on the SCR, we do not provide concrete cutoffs or point requirements regarding which students should be recommended for special services.** Rather, the SCR is intended to flag students for scaffolded services and to enable them to reach their potential. It also provides a way to monitor and record students' behaviors.

What follows is an explanation of the categories and items included on the SCR, along with some examples of how the specified student behaviors might be evidenced in your classroom.

Engagement

1. **Student arrives in class with new ideas to bring to the project that he or she has thought of outside of class.** New ideas may manifest themselves as ideas about how to approach a problem, about new research information found on the Internet or elsewhere outside of class, about something in the news or in the paper that is relevant to the subject, or about a connection between the subject and an observed behavior.

2. **Student shares ideas with a small group of peers, but may fade into the background in front of a larger group.** The student may rise to be a leader when the small group is working on a project, but if asked to get up in front of the class, then that student fades into the background and lets others do the talking.

3. **Student engagement results in a marked increase in the quality of his or her performance.** This is particularly evident in a student who does not normally engage in class at all. During the unit, the student suddenly becomes engaged and produces something amazing.

4. **Student eagerly interacts with appropriate questions, but may be reluctant to put things down on paper.** This is an example of a loophole behavior, or one that causes a student to be overlooked when teachers and specialists are identifying giftedness. It is particularly evident in students who live in largely "oral" worlds, which is to say that they communicate best verbally and are often frustrated by written methods, or in those who have writing disabilities.

Creativity

1. **Student intuitively makes "leaps" in his or her thinking.** Occasionally, you will be explaining something, and a lightbulb will go on for a student, causing him or her to take the concept far beyond the content being covered. Although there are students who do this with regularity, it is more often an intensity behavior, meaning that when it occurs, the student is very intense in his or her thinking, creativity, reasoning, and so on. This can be tricky to identify, because often, the student is unable to explain his or her thinking, and the teacher realizes only later that a leap in understanding was achieved.

2. **Student makes up new rules, words, or protocols to express his or her own ideas.** This can take various forms, one of which is a student's taking two words and literally combining them to try to express what he or she is thinking about. Other times, a student will want to change the rules to make his or her idea possible.

3. **Student thinks on his or her feet in response to a project challenge, to make excuses, or to extend his or her work.** This is another loophole

behavior, because it often occurs when a student is being defensive or even misbehaving, making a teacher less likely to interpret it as evidence of giftedness. It is sometimes on display during classroom debates and discussions.

4. **Student uses pictures or other inventive means to illustrate his or her ideas.** Given the choice, this student would rather draw an idea than put it into words. This could take the shape of the student creating a character web or a design idea. The student might also act out an idea or use objects to demonstrate understanding.

Synthesis

1. **Student goes above and beyond directions to expand ideas.** It is wonderful to behold this behavior in students, particularly when displayed by those students who are rarely engaged. A student may be excited about a given idea and keep generating increasingly creative or complex material to expand upon that idea. For instance, we had a student who, during the mock trial unit, became intrigued by forensic evidence and decided to generate and interpret evidence to bolster his team's case.

2. **Student has strong opinions on projects, but may struggle to accept directions that contradict his or her opinions.** This student may understand directions, but be unwilling to yield to an idea that conflicts with his or her own idea. This behavior, rather than indicating a lack of understanding, is typical of students with strong ideas.

3. **Student is comfortable processing new ideas.** This behavior is evident in students who take new ideas and quickly extend them or ask insightful questions.

4. **Student blends new and old ideas.** This behavior has to do with processing a new idea, retrieving an older idea, and relating the two to one another. For instance, a student who learns about using string to measure distance might remember making a treasure map and extrapolate that a string would have been useful for taking into account curves and winding paths.

Interpersonal Ability

1. **Student is an academic leader who, when engaged, increases his or her levels of investment and enthusiasm in the group.** This is a student who has so much enthusiasm for learning that he or she makes the project engaging for the whole group, fostering an attitude of motivation or optimism.

2. **Student is a social leader in the classroom, but may not be an academic leader.** To observe this type of behavior, you may have to be vigilant, for some students are disengaged in the classroom but come alive as soon as they cross the threshold into the hallway, where they can socialize with their

peers. Often, this student is able to get the rest of the group to do whatever he or she wants (and does not necessarily use this talent for good).

3. **Student works through group conflict to enable the group to complete its work.** When the group has a conflict, this is the student who solves the problem or addresses the issue so that the group can get back to work. This is an interpersonal measure, and thus, it does not describe a student who simply elects to do all of the work rather than confronting his or her peers about sharing the load.

4. **Student is a Tom Sawyer in classroom situations, using his or her charm to get others to do the work.** There is an important distinction to watch out for when identifying this type of behavior: You must be sure that the student is *not* a bully, coercing others to do his or her work. Instead, this student actually makes other students *want* to lend a helping hand. For instance, a twice-exceptional student who is highly talented but struggles with reading might develop charm in order to get other students to transpose his verbally expressed ideas into writing.

Verbal Communication

1. **Participation in brainstorming sessions (e.g., group work) increases student's productivity.** When this type of student is given the opportunity to verbally process with peers, he or she is often able to come up with the answer. For instance, if asked outright for an answer, this student may shrug, but if given a minute to consult with a neighbor, then the student usually is able and willing to offer the correct answer.

2. **Student constructively disagrees with peers and/or the teacher by clearly sharing his or her thoughts.** This student can defend his or her point of view with examples and reasoning—not just in a formal debate, but also in general classroom situations. He or she has learned to channel thoughts into constructive disagreement, rather than flying off the handle merely to win an argument.

3. **Student verbally expresses his or her academic and/or social needs.** This student can speak up when confused or experiencing personality clashes within a group. This student knows when to ask for help and can clearly articulate what help is needed.

4. **Student uses strong word choice and a variety of tones to bring expression to his or her verbal communication.** This student is an engaging speaker and speaks loudly and clearly enough for everybody to hear. A wide vocabulary is also indicative that this student's verbal capability is exceptional.

Student: _____

Date: _____

Fill out the rubric according to what you have observed about each student's behaviors. Then, for each area, record the number of items you marked "Not observed," "Sometimes," and "Often." Multiply these tallies by the corresponding point values (0, 1, and 2) to get the totals for each area. There is an option to check for high intensity so you can better keep track of students' behaviors.

STUDENT CONTEXT RUBRIC

ENGAGEMENT

1. Student arrives in class with new ideas to bring to the project that he or she has thought of outside of class.
   NOT OBSERVED　SOMETIMES　OFTEN　HIGH INTENSITY

2. Student shares ideas with a small group of peers, but may fade into the background in front of a larger group.
   NOT OBSERVED　SOMETIMES　OFTEN　HIGH INTENSITY

3. Student engagement results in a marked increase in the quality of his or her performance.
   NOT OBSERVED　SOMETIMES　OFTEN　HIGH INTENSITY

4. Student eagerly interacts with appropriate questions, but may be reluctant to put things down on paper.
   NOT OBSERVED　SOMETIMES　OFTEN　HIGH INTENSITY

CREATIVITY

1. Student intuitively makes "leaps" in his or her thinking.
   NOT OBSERVED　SOMETIMES　OFTEN　HIGH INTENSITY

2. Student makes up new rules, words, or protocols to express his or her own ideas.
   NOT OBSERVED　SOMETIMES　OFTEN　HIGH INTENSITY

3. Student thinks on his or her feet in response to a project challenge, to make excuses, or to extend his or her work.
   NOT OBSERVED　SOMETIMES　OFTEN　HIGH INTENSITY

4. Student uses pictures or other inventive means to illustrate his or her ideas.
   NOT OBSERVED　SOMETIMES　OFTEN　HIGH INTENSITY

SYNTHESIS

1. Student goes above and beyond directions to expand ideas.
   NOT OBSERVED　SOMETIMES　OFTEN　HIGH INTENSITY

2. Student has strong opinions on projects, but may struggle to accept directions that contradict his or her opinions.
   NOT OBSERVED　SOMETIMES　OFTEN　HIGH INTENSITY

3. Student is comfortable processing new ideas.
   NOT OBSERVED　SOMETIMES　OFTEN　HIGH INTENSITY

4. Student blends new ideas and old ideas.
   NOT OBSERVED　SOMETIMES　OFTEN　HIGH INTENSITY

INTERPERSONAL ABILITY

1. Student is an academic leader who, when engaged, increases his or her levels of investment and enthusiasm in the group.
   NOT OBSERVED　SOMETIMES　OFTEN　HIGH INTENSITY

2. Student is a social leader in the classroom, but may not be an academic leader.
   NOT OBSERVED　SOMETIMES　OFTEN　HIGH INTENSITY

3. Student works through group conflict to enable the group to complete its work.
   NOT OBSERVED　SOMETIMES　OFTEN　HIGH INTENSITY

4. Student is a Tom Sawyer in classroom situations, using his or her charm to get others to do the work.
   NOT OBSERVED　SOMETIMES　OFTEN　HIGH INTENSITY

VERBAL COMMUNICATION

1. Participation in brainstorming sessions (e.g., group work) increases student's productivity.
   NOT OBSERVED　SOMETIMES　OFTEN　HIGH INTENSITY

2. Student constructively disagrees with peers and/or the teacher by clearly sharing his or her thoughts.
   NOT OBSERVED　SOMETIMES　OFTEN　HIGH INTENSITY

3. Student verbally expresses his or her academic and/or social needs.
   NOT OBSERVED　SOMETIMES　OFTEN　HIGH INTENSITY

4. Student uses strong word choice and a variety of tones to bring expression to his or her verbal communication.
   NOT OBSERVED　SOMETIMES　OFTEN　HIGH INTENSITY

AREA	NOT 0	SOME 1	OFTEN 2	HIGH	TOTAL
ENGAGEMENT					
CREATIVITY					
SYNTHESIS					
INTERPERSONAL ABILITY					
VERBAL COMMUNICATION					
ADD TOTALS					

Developed by Cote & Blauvelt under the auspices of the Further Steps Forward Project, a Jacob Javits grant program, #S206A050086.

About the Authors

Darcy O. Blauvelt has been teaching in a variety of facilities for more than 12 years. Her educational journey has included public schools, private schools, nursery schools, and a professional theatre for children ages 3–18. Blauvelt holds educational certification in Theatre K–12, Early Childhood Education, and English Education 5–12. She holds a B.A. in theatre from Chatham College, Pittsburgh, PA, and has done graduate work at Lesley University in Massachusetts in creative arts in learning, as well as at Millersville University in Pennsylvania in psychology.

In 2005, she joined the Nashua School District as a gifted and talented resource specialist. Subsequently, she served full time as the program coordinator for the Further Steps Forward Project, a Javits Grant program, from 2005–2009. Blauvelt returned to the classroom in the fall of 2009 and currently teaches seventh-grade English in Nashua, NH. Blauvelt lives in Manchester, NH, with her husband, two dogs, five cats, and the occasional son!

Richard G. Cote, M.B.A., is a career educator. He has dedicated 41 years to being a classroom teacher (mathematics, physics), a community college adjunct instructor (economics), a gifted and talented resource specialist, and the director of the Further Steps Forward Project, a Javits Grant program.

His development of the MESH (mathematics, English, science, and history) program has led him to several audiences. He has presented at various national conventions, civic/community groups, district school boards, teacher organizations, community colleges, and universities, and has served as a consultant to educators throughout the country. Cote helped develop the teacher certification examination for physics at the Institute for Educational Testing and Research at the University of South Florida. He completed the Florida Council on Educational Management Program in Educational Leadership, and he is the recipient of numerous awards, including a certificate of merit on economics education from the University of South Florida, a grant from the Florida Council on Economics Education, a Florida Compact award, and a prestigious NAGC Curriculum Studies award for the development of *Ecopolis* and *What's Your Opinion?*

Now retired from the workplace, Cote continues to share his energy, creativity, and expertise with educators through the Interactive Discovery-Based Units for High-Ability Learners.

Common Core State Standards Alignment

Grade Level	Common Core State Standards in ELA-Literacy
Grade 6 ELA-Literacy	W.6.1 Write arguments to support claims with clear reasons and relevant evidence. W.6.2 Write informative/explanatory texts to examine a topic and convey ideas, concepts, and information through the selection, organization, and analysis of relevant content. W.6.4 Produce clear and coherent writing in which the development, organization, and style are appropriate to task, purpose, and audience. (Grade-specific expectations for writing types are defined in standards 1–3 above.) W.6.5 With some guidance and support from peers and adults, develop and strengthen writing as needed by planning, revising, editing, rewriting, or trying a new approach. (Editing for conventions should demonstrate command of Language standards 1–3 up to and including grade 6 here.)

Grade Level	Common Core State Standards in ELA-Literacy
Grade 6 ELA-Literacy *continued*	SL.6.1 Engage effectively in a range of collaborative discussions (one-on-one, in groups, and teacher-led) with diverse partners on grade 6 topics, texts, and issues, building on others' ideas and expressing their own clearly. SL.6.2 Interpret information presented in diverse media and formats (e.g., visually, quantitatively, orally) and explain how it contributes to a topic, text, or issue under study. SL.6.3 Delineate a speaker's argument and specific claims, distinguishing claims that are supported by reasons and evidence from claims that are not. SL.6.4 Present claims and findings, sequencing ideas logically and using pertinent descriptions, facts, and details to accentuate main ideas or themes; use appropriate eye contact, adequate volume, and clear pronunciation. SL.6.6 Adapt speech to a variety of contexts and tasks, demonstrating command of formal English when indicated or appropriate. (See grade 6 Language standards 1 and 3 here for specific expectations.) L.6.1 Demonstrate command of the conventions of standard English grammar and usage when writing or speaking. L.6.3 Use knowledge of language and its conventions when writing, speaking, reading, or listening. L.6.4 Determine or clarify the meaning of unknown and multiple-meaning words and phrases based on grade 6 reading and content, choosing flexibly from a range of strategies. L.6.6 Acquire and use accurately grade-appropriate general academic and domain-specific words and phrases; gather vocabulary knowledge when considering a word or phrase important to comprehension or expression.
Grade 7 ELA-Literacy	W.7.1 Write arguments to support claims with clear reasons and relevant evidence. W.7.2 Write informative/explanatory texts to examine a topic and convey ideas, concepts, and information through the selection, organization, and analysis of relevant content. W.7.4 Produce clear and coherent writing in which the development, organization, and style are appropriate to task, purpose, and audience. (Grade-specific expectations for writing types are defined in standards 1–3 above.)

Grade Level	Common Core State Standards in ELA-Literacy
Grade 7 ELA-Literacy *continued*	W.7.5 With some guidance and support from peers and adults, develop and strengthen writing as needed by planning, revising, editing, rewriting, or trying a new approach, focusing on how well purpose and audience have been addressed. (Editing for conventions should demonstrate command of Language standards 1–3 up to and including grade 7 here.) SL.7.1 Engage effectively in a range of collaborative discussions (one-on-one, in groups, and teacher-led) with diverse partners on grade 7 topics, texts, and issues, building on others' ideas and expressing their own clearly. SL.7.2 Analyze the main ideas and supporting details presented in diverse media and formats (e.g., visually, quantitatively, orally) and explain how the ideas clarify a topic, text, or issue under study. SL.7.3 Delineate a speaker's argument and specific claims, evaluating the soundness of the reasoning and the relevance and sufficiency of the evidence. SL.7.4 Present claims and findings, emphasizing salient points in a focused, coherent manner with pertinent descriptions, facts, details, and examples; use appropriate eye contact, adequate volume, and clear pronunciation. SL.7.6 Adapt speech to a variety of contexts and tasks, demonstrating command of formal English when indicated or appropriate. (See grade 7 Language standards 1 and 3 here for specific expectations.) L.7.1 Demonstrate command of the conventions of standard English grammar and usage when writing or speaking. L.7.3 Use knowledge of language and its conventions when writing, speaking, reading, or listening. L.7.4 Determine or clarify the meaning of unknown and multiple-meaning words and phrases based on grade 7 reading and content, choosing flexibly from a range of strategies. L.7.6 Acquire and use accurately grade-appropriate general academic and domain-specific words and phrases; gather vocabulary knowledge when considering a word or phrase important to comprehension or expression.
Grade 8 ELA-Literacy	W.8.1 Write arguments to support claims with clear reasons and relevant evidence.

Grade Level	Common Core State Standards in ELA-Literacy
Grade 8 ELA-Literacy *continued*	W.8.2 Write informative/explanatory texts to examine a topic and convey ideas, concepts, and information through the selection, organization, and analysis of relevant content. W.8.4 Produce clear and coherent writing in which the development, organization, and style are appropriate to task, purpose, and audience. (Grade-specific expectations for writing types are defined in standards 1–3 above.) W.8.5 With some guidance and support from peers and adults, develop and strengthen writing as needed by planning, revising, editing, rewriting, or trying a new approach, focusing on how well purpose and audience have been addressed. (Editing for conventions should demonstrate command of Language standards 1–3 up to and including grade 8 here.) SL.8.1 Engage effectively in a range of collaborative discussions (one-on-one, in groups, and teacher-led) with diverse partners on grade 8 topics, texts, and issues, building on others' ideas and expressing their own clearly. SL.8.2 Analyze the purpose of information presented in diverse media and formats (e.g., visually, quantitatively, orally) and evaluate the motives (e.g., social, commercial, political) behind its presentation. SL.8.3 Delineate a speaker's argument and specific claims, evaluating the soundness of the reasoning and relevance and sufficiency of the evidence and identifying when irrelevant evidence is introduced. SL.8.4 Present claims and findings, emphasizing salient points in a focused, coherent manner with relevant evidence, sound valid reasoning, and well-chosen details; use appropriate eye contact, adequate volume, and clear pronunciation. SL.8.6 Adapt speech to a variety of contexts and tasks, demonstrating command of formal English when indicated or appropriate. (See grade 8 Language standards 1 and 3 here for specific expectations.) L.8.1 Demonstrate command of the conventions of standard English grammar and usage when writing or speaking. L.8.3 Use knowledge of language and its conventions when writing, speaking, reading, or listening. L.8.4 Determine or clarify the meaning of unknown and multiple-meaning words or phrases based on grade 8 reading and content, choosing flexibly from a range of strategies.

Grade Level	Common Core State Standards in ELA-Literacy
Grade 8 ELA-Literacy *continued*	L.8.6 Acquire and use accurately grade-appropriate general academic and domain-specific words and phrases; gather vocabulary knowledge when considering a word or phrase important to comprehension or expression.
Grades 6-8 ELA-Literacy	RH.6-8.2 Determine the central ideas or information of a primary or secondary source; provide an accurate summary of the source distinct from prior knowledge or opinions. RH.6-8.3 Identify key steps in a text's description of a process related to history/social studies (e.g., how a bill becomes law, how interest rates are raised or lowered). RH.6-8.4 Determine the meaning of words and phrases as they are used in a text, including vocabulary specific to domains related to history/social studies. RH.6-8.5 Describe how a text presents information (e.g., sequentially, comparatively, causally). RH.6-8.6 Identify aspects of a text that reveal an author's point of view or purpose (e.g., loaded language, inclusion or avoidance of particular facts). RH.6-8.8 Distinguish among fact, opinion, and reasoned judgment in a text. RH.6-8.9 Analyze the relationship between a primary and secondary source on the same topic. RH.6-8.10 By the end of grade 8, read and comprehend history/social studies texts in the grades 6–8 text complexity band independently and proficiently.

For Product Safety Concerns and Information please contact our EU representative GPSR@taylorandfrancis.com Taylor & Francis Verlag GmbH, Kaufingerstraße 24, 80331 München, Germany